SPANISH VERBS, SIMPLIFIED

SPANISH VERBS, SIMPLIFIED

Luis Toral Moreno

Para realizar pedidos de este libro, contacte con:
Palibrio
1663 Liberty Drive, Suite 200
Bloomington, IN 47403
Gratis desde EE. UU. al 877.407.5847
Gratis desde México al 01.800.288.2243
Gratis desde España al 900.866.949
Desde otro país al +1.812.671.9757
Fax: 01.812.355.1576
ventas@palibrio.com
663560

Contents

Preface vii
List of Abbreviations ix
Pronunciation of vowels and diphtongs..................................... xiii
Syllabication xv
Written Accent xvi

PART I — ONE SINGLE TABLE for the
Conjugation of ALL the Spanish Verbs

Introduction I
Definitions 2
A Complete Conjugation..5
Usage of Tú and Usted, and of Vosotros and Ustedes.............8
Meaning and Usage of the Tenses...9
Composition and use of the single TABLE 14
Table I...17
Table I...19
Drills for getting acquainted with the TABLE.........................21

PART 2 — A Separate Study of Each Irregularity

Introduction 23
Table 2.. 27
Table 3.. 27
Illustrative Examples for Table 3 29
Changes in Spelling 30
Irregularities in the Present... 32
    GU Irregularity 32
    DI Irregularity..33
    VO irregularity 36
    YE irregularity 38
Verbs with a double Irregularity in the Present....................... 39
Irregularities in the Past... 42
    PI irregularity...42
    VO irregularity 44
    NI irregularity..46

Irregularities in the Future.. 47
    FI irregularity.. 47
Irregularities of the Tu Imp... 49
Irregularities of the Gerund... 50
Irregularities in the past participle 51
Table 4... 54
Peculiar irregularities of the MO Verbs 56
Table 5... 60
Verbs ending in iar and uar.. 61
Defective verbs.. 62
General List of Irregular Verbs.. 65

PREFACE

From the faraway year of 1911, when I began to learn English and French, I became interested in a comparative examination of the different languages. And since then, and all along my life, I have always enjoyed, not as a serious study but as a pleasant hobby, to become aware of the peculiarities of whatever tongues I have been able to study.

It is natural, then, that in the case of the Spanish verbs, my attention has been so attracted by the most remarkable simplicity and regularity of their conjugation as compared to the conjugation of the regular and irregular verbs of Latin, Greek, French and Italian; being mentioned only these four languages not to meddle into the complication of the Arabic and Hebrew verbs.

Being the verb the most important part of speech, the essential element of every sentence, all grammarians have been much more preoccupied of the syntactic rather than of its purely physical aspects. In all the books I have read I have not yet found that the two points which are the principal basis of this work of mine have been specially developed. Far from me to think that my idea is original. All grammarians have handled these points, but no one has specially singled them out. No one has put distinctive emphasis on them.

The two parts composing the present work, i.e., the two points that I wish to develop are:

1) The composition and use of ONE SINGLE TABLE that can serve for the conjugation of all the Spanish verbs, both regular and irregular. With this TABLE a much easier, simpler way of learning how to conjugate any Spanish verb is attained.
2) The separate study of each class of irregularity, grouping the irregularities by tenses and in a minimum of classes. By this method a more logic, much easier and simpler way of learning all the irregular Spanish verbs is attained.

As I am not a scholar at all, I had never thought possible or worthwhile to put in writing, and still less to publish, my cogitations on this matter. But as I have always been in the habit of talking about these topics to my relatives and friends and even to anybody who showed some interest in the matter, there have been many people who, half jokingly, half seriously, have induced and encourage me to finally publish in Spanish this work.

I have also ventured the thought that it could be useful to publish in English a short treatise based on those two points and in which the simplicity and regularity of the Spanish conjugation would be persistently shown. Although I do not intend or pretend to do an exhaustive study of the Spanish verbs, it might be almost useless, for an English speaking reader who is trying to learn Spanish, if this paper would be limited to develop those two points. I have endeavored to include, within the most possible shortness, the essential things of the conjugation, to wit, the meaning and usage of the tenses, so it could merit the title of

"Spanish Verbs, Simplified"

A MOST IMPORTANT NOTICE

I insist in stating that it is <u>entirely fundamental</u>, for the understanding of this work, to get well acquainted with the list of abbreviations, this being obtained after just a few minutes studying it. I have found out that most of my readers, if acquainted with the abbreviations, have met their use to become advantageous, natural and easy. But if they do not know how to interpret and use my abbreviations, this work seems to them complicated and hard to understand. I tried to make all abbreviations easily pronounceable and obviously understandable.

N.B. My abbreviations should of course be pronounced as if they were Spanish words. For instance, <u>Tu</u> is to be pronounced (Too); <u>Seis</u> is to be pronounced (Sayss).

LIST OF ABBREVIATIONS

Abbreviations have always been considered useful and convenient. They are used to avoid repetition of long, cumbersome words or phrases. They are used for citing the Bible books. There is at the beginning of all dictionaries an enormous list of abbreviations. They are irreplaceable for the mathematical and chemical formulas. Modern trends have multiplied the use of abbreviated symbols: For chemical compounds, DDT is used instead of <u>d</u>ichlor<u>d</u>iphenyl<u>t</u>richlorethane; TNT is used instead of <u>t</u>rini<u>t</u>rotoluene. For international agencies, UNESCO is used instead of <u>U</u>nited <u>N</u>ations <u>E</u>ducational, <u>S</u>cientific and <u>C</u>ultural <u>O</u>rganization.

It must not be strange, therefore, that I have decided to make an ample use of abbreviations in this work. Evidently much time and effort (and even paper and ink) are saved if instead of writing and reading <u>first person, singular, indicative present</u>, just <u>Yo Pres</u> is used.

For persons:

| Yo | - | first person, singular | <u>Yo</u> (I) |
| Tu | - | second person, singular | <u>Tú</u> (familiar you) |

El	-	third person, singular	Él (he)
Nos	-	first person, plural	Nosotros (we)
Vos	-	second person, plural	Vosotros (plural you)
Els	-	third person, plural	Ellos (they)
Qua	-	the four (cuatro) persons (Yo, Tu, El, Els) of the Pres (and the SuPres) of the Spanish verbs.	
		They are called the strong forms because the stem, instead of ending, bears the stress: ´gan.o, ´gan.as, etc. Three classes of the irregular verbs have an irregular Qua in the Pres.	
Seis	-	the six (seis) persons of a tense, i.e., the whole tense. Many tenses of the irregular verbs are Seis.	

For tenses: (Names of the tenses are those given by BELLO)

Pres	-	presente (present)	indicative	cant.as	you sing
Pas	-	pretérito (past)	indicative	cant.aste	you sang
Fu	-	futuro (future)	indicative	cantar.ás	you will sing
Co	-	copretérito (imperfect)	indicative	cant.abas	you were singing
Pos	-	pospretérito (conditional)	indicative	cantar.ías	you would sing
Imp	-	presente (present)	imperative	cant.a	sing
SuPres	-	presente (present)	subjunctive	cant.es	(that) you sing
SuPas	-	pretérito (past)	subjunctive	cant.aras	(if) you would sing
SuFu	-	futuro (future)	subjunctive	cant.ares	(if) you ever would sing
Inf	-	infinitivo (infinitive)	verbals	cant.ar	(to) sing

Ger	-	gerundio	verbals	cant.	singing
		(gerund)		ando	
Par	-	participio	verbals	cant.ado	sung
		(past			
		participle)			

For classes of irregularities:

GU - a guttural sound is added to the stem: from nacer, nazco; from caer,

caigo; from tener, tengo, etc.

DI - a vowel of the stem is changed into a diphtong: from pensar, pienso; from

rodar, ruedo; from adquirir, adquiero; from jugar, juego; etc.

VO - a vowel of the stem is changed into another vowel: from pedir, pido,

pidió; from morir, muramos, muriendo; etc.

YE - a y (a ye sound) is added to the stem: from inclu.ir, incluy. amos,

instead of inclu.amos, from o.ír, oy.es, instead of o.es; etc.

PI - irregular (strong) past: from pon.er, ´pus.e, instead of pon.í; from

tener, ´tuv.o, instead of ten.ió; etc.

FI - irregular future; a certain change is made to the stem (the whole

infinitive): from poder, poder.é, podré; from decir, diré; etc.

NI - an i is taken out from the ending (of El and Els Pas and imitating

tenses): from gruñir, gruñ.ió; from reír, ri.ieron, rieron; etc.

MO - six verbs (the only Spanish verbs with a monosyllabic Pres) having

such peculiar irregularities that they merit to be classified and

studied in a special group (BELLO did so): dar, (e)star, haber,

ser, ver, ir.

For endings of verbal forms:

Tem - the mood-tense morpheme, first part of the ending of all
verbal forms:
from cant.ar, cant.aba s, cant.ára mos, cantar.ía n, etc.

Pen - the person-number morpheme, second part of the ending of all
verbal forms:
from cant.ar, cant.aba s, cant.ára mos, cantar.ía n, etc.

Other abbreviations:

col   - column
Conj 1   - conjugation one, of verbs ending in ar: cantar, pensar, etc.
Conj 2   - conjugation two, of verbs ending in er: comer, poder, etc.
Conj 3   - conjugation three, of verbs ending in ir: vivir, decir, etc.
Irr   - irregular
R   - regular

A diagonal line over a letter (s) means that this letter must be omitted. It is sometimes put to call the attention on a certain feature.

For bibliography: (Only the following authorities will be cited)

ENGLE - Esbozo de una Nueva Gramática de la Lengua Española (Outline of a new Grammar of the Spanish Language) – by the Grammar Commission of the Royal Spanish Academy (a recognized supreme authority on Spanish grammar matters) – Espasa-Calpe, Madrid, 1975 – chapters 2.10 to 2.15.

BELLO   -   Gramática de la Lengua Castellana (Grammar of the Castilian (Spanish) Language) – by Andrés <u>Bello</u> (the recognized best grammarian) – R. Roger & F. Chernoviz, Editors, Paris, 1913 – chapters XXIV to XXVI.

When TABLE (in capital letters) is written, it specifically means Table One, i.e., the single table for conjugation of <u>all</u> Spanish verbs. When the "Academia" is mentioned, it means the dictionary or the grammar of the Royal Spanish Academy (of the Language).

When "in Mexico" is written, meaning that something is used or is <u>not</u> used in Mexico, it is not intended to say: exclusively in Mexico. Maybe it is used or not used in many or several of the Spanish speaking regions. I employ this expression because this paper is specially devoted to Mexico.

A FEW HINTS ON PRONUNCIATION

Pronunciation of vowels and diphtongs

Spanish pronunciation is so regular and easy that there is no <u>good</u> Spanish-English dictionary that has to use a system of pronunciation. But I have seen that almost all popular methods for teaching Spanish to English speaking people give false and absurd systems of pronunciation. For instance, the pronunciation of <u>bueno</u> is given as boo.´ayn.oh. So I thought it would be useful to devote a few lines to the pronunciation of Spanish vowels and diphtongs.

For all practical purposes it can be said that there are in Spanish <u>only</u> a five vowel sounds, i.e., each vowel is pronounced nearly identically regardless of the position it occupies in the word. There are grammars and methods which indicate that the Spanish <u>e</u> is pronounced <u>more</u> openly in p<u>e</u>rro and p<u>e</u>rla than in p<u>e</u>lo and m<u>e</u>sa. But my opinion is that if an American pronounces <u>any</u> Spanish <u>e</u> as the <u>e</u> in the English word <u>press</u>, he is pronouncing it much better than if he is trying to distinguish the different shades.

The following are the pronunciations I deem acceptable for the Spanish vowels:

a   -   (palabra, Guadalajara), as the a sound in mine, cow, I, sound, etc.

e   -   (siete, eterno), as the e sound in press, best, etc.

i   -   (divino, máquina), as the i sound in machine, queen, etc.

o   -   (corto, oportuno), as the o sound in toy, already, etc.

u   -   (susurro, columna), as the u sound in soon, clue, etc.

In Spanish, a, e, and o are called strong vowels, and i and u are called weak vowels. The combination of a strong vowel and a weak vowel into a single syllable (cai, cuo, cau, quie, etc.) is called a diphtong. In English, two vowels are frequently pronounced separately (re.ality, tru.ant, pictori.al, situ.ate). But in Spanish (specially in Mexico), they must be pronounced forming one syllable: the weak vowel takes a consonant sound for becoming a diphtong (quieto, kietto; reina, rayna; bueno, bwenno) as in English boy, yes, queen, etc. When the two vowels are to be pronounced separately, undoing the diphtong, it is always indicated by an accent (´) as it is explained in rule 3) of the accentuation rules given later under "Written Accent" (ma.íz, a.ún, ca.í.da, etc.).

The following are the pronunciations I deem acceptable for the 14 Spanish diphtongs:

ai, ay   -   (aire, hay), as in side, my.

ei, ey   -   (peine, rey), as in table, say.

oi, oy   -   (oigo, soy), as in coin, boy.

au   -   (causa, aplaudir), as in round, cow.

eu   -   (Europa, neutro), there is no such sound in English. It is to be

pronounced like every (´evry) if v would be changed into w (´ewry).

ou   -   (Sousa), as in low. (Used only in Portuguese and Catalonian Family

names).

ia, ya   -   (copia, raya), as in yarn.

ie, ye	-	(cielo, hielo, yeso), as in yes, yet.
io, yo	-	(acción, coyote), as in yawn, fjord.
iu, yu	-	(viuda, yugo), as in few, you.
ua, hua	-	(igual, cacahuate), as the wa sound in wine, twine.
ue, hue	-	(bueno, hueso), as in twenty, west.
ui, hui	-	(ciudado, huizache), as in queen, we.
uo	-	(cuota), as in quotation.
uy	-	(muy), as in ruin. A very special case, the u bears the stress.

Syllabication

Words are divided into syllables in a different manner in Spanish than in English. In Spanish, ca.len.da.rio, pé.ta.lo, a.ná.lo.go, pe.ró.xi.do, etc. In English, cal.endar, pet.al, na.alog, per.ox.ide, etc.

Let us call a single consonant the consonant constituted by one single letter; a double consonant the consonants ch, ll or rr which represent one sound only; and a compound consonant the consonants b, c, d, f, g, p or t followed by l or r: bra, cle, dri, flo, gru, etc.

A single consonant (including x and y) between two vowels is always pronounced and written with the following vowel (never with the former vowel): pa.no.rá.mi.co, clá.si.co, pa.ya.so, etc. If there are two single consonants between the two vowels, the second one is pronounced and written with the following vowel: pres.tan.do, etc. If it is a double or compound consonant, it is of course attached to the following vowel: di.cho, po.llo, pe.rro, me.tro, chi.cle, etc.

If there are three consonants between two vowels and the second and third ones form a double or compound consonant, these two are attached to the following vowel: con.cha, cos.tra, etc. But if all three are single consonants, only the third one is attached to the following vowel: ist.mo, pers.pirar, ins.pector, obs.curo, etc.

If there are four consonants, the third and the fourth ones always form a compound consonant which is of course pronounced with and attached to the following vowel: ins.tructor, mens.truación, etc.

Notice that for the examples given in the latter two paragraphs the second consonant is almost always an s. Contrary to the strictest English rule, this s is pronounced and written in Spanish togehter with the first consonant. Our language never admits a liquid s even when the etymology might exact it: Spanish, pers.pirar, cons.ciente, cons.tructivo; English, per.spire, con.scious, con.structive.

Written Accent

In English, and in many other languages, it is necessary to learn, for each word, which syllable bears the stress, because it is never shown by a written mark. While in Spanish, by the use of a written accent (´), it is always ascertained which syllable of any word, even if its meaning is not know, bears the stress.

A word is called aguda (oxytone) if the stress is on the last syllable (cantará); grave (paroxytone) if the stress is on the next to last syllable (cantara); esdrújula (proparoxytone) if the stress is before the last two syllables (cántara, último).

It was verified that more than 80 per cent of the Spanish words (of more than one syllable) are grave (paroxytone) which end in a vowel or in n or s. Based on this finding, the Academia has established the following set of rules, the most simple and without any exceptions, for the use of a written accent.

1) No accent is needed for a grave word ending in a vowel or in n or s (casa, come, casi, comen, comes, etc.) No accent is needed for an aguda word ending in any consonant other than n or s (vivac, salud, reloj, igual, temor, feroz, etc.)

2) On the contrary: Any grave word must be marked with a written accent if it ends in any consonant other than n or s (cárcel, mártir, lápiz, etc.). Any aguda word must be

marked with a written accent if it ends in a vowel or in n or s (mamá, café, bisturí, mansión, escribirás, etc.). Any esdrújula must be marked with a written accent (máscara, próximo, lápices, dígame, etc.). By the way, if a diphtong has to be accented, the accent must be marked on the strong vowel (acción, ganáis, áureo, etc.)

3) Contrary to rule 1): A word must be marked with the accent on an i or a u which bears the stress and is accompanied by another vowel not forming a diphtong: vario is not accented, varí.o must be accented; Cairo is not accented, ca.ído must be accented; etc.)

To sum it up, a foreginer (or any person) can be sure of pronouncing correctly any Spanish word, even if he does not know its meaning. If it bears a written accent he knows where the stress is. If there is no written accent he knows it is a grave word if it ends in a vowel of in n or s. He knows it is an aguda word if it ends in a consonant which is other than n or s.

N.B. No accent is needed for one-syllable words. A few words bear a written accent to be distinguished from another word spelled alike; tú (you), tu (your); él (he), el (the); sí (yes), si (if); mí (me), mi (my); dé (give), de (of); cuándo (interrogative), cuando (affirmative), etc.

PART ONE

ONE SINGLE TABLE for the Conjugation of ALL the Spanish Verbs

Introduction

For many many years I had been pondering on the possibility of a much simpler, much easier, less bulky manner of studying the conjugations, since Spanish positively possesses a most remarkably regular and uniform way of conjugating all verbs, both regular and irregular. All grammars employ pages and more pages in paradigms of the conjugations of regular verbs, and then more and more pages for the description of numerous groups or classes of verbs of common irregularities and of odd verbs with special irregularities. The true reason for continuing to do so is, I think, what BELLO writes in his Preface: The excessive admiration everybody has had for the Latin is the cause why we have kept using for our language the nomenclature and the grammatical rules of Latin. It might also be an imitation of how verbs are classified in some modern languages, like French.

It is undeniable, of course, that for the study of the Spanish grammar it is essential to take into account what the philology, the linguistics, the etymology, the comparative grammar teach. But if Spanish has, fortunately, regularized and simplified so much its conjugations, let us forget how verbs were conjugated in Latin or how verbs are classified and conjugated in other modern languages. Let us confine ourselves to study how easy the verbal forms are now in Spanish.

By tradition, and because in Latin there are four conjugations, one in are, two in ere, and one in ire, all grammarians consider in Spanish three conjugations: Conj 1 in ar (gan.ar), Conj. 2 in er (com. er), Conj. 3 in ir (viv.ir). But also all grammarians point out that the conjugations are practically reduced to only two, because Conj 2 and Conj 3, aside from the Inf ending (com.er, viv.ir), have only three other differences (all in the Tem morpheme only): Nos Pre, com.e.mos, viv.i.mos; Vos Pres, com.é.is, viv.i.ís; Vos Imp, com.e.d., viv.i.d (the last two are not used in Mexico any more). Maybe it is convenient anyway to retain the difference because two of the classes of irregularities, VO and YE, occur exclusively on verbs of Conj 3 (VO pedir, YE hui).

All verbal forms are composed of two parts: the stem and the ending. The stem, in the regular verbs, remains without any variation all along the whole conjugation. In the irregular verbs it is modified according to very precise rules as shown in Table 3.

The Tem morpheme of the ending remains unchanged, in <u>all</u> verbs, for the <u>six</u> persons of each tense, except for a few and very precise exceptions.

The Pen morpheme of the ending remains unchanged for each person in <u>all</u> tenses of <u>all</u> verbs, except for a few and very precise exceptions.

That is why I have estimated that it turns out useless, if not detrimental, to entangle things with numerous paradigms of conjugations, being sufficient to make up <u>one single table</u> for the conjugation of <u>all</u> the simple tenses of <u>all</u> the Spanish verbs, both regular and irregular.

This is perfectly attained by TABLE I.

Definitions

(The outstanding purpose of this list is the comparison between Spanish and English terms)

Oración –
Sentence: A combination of words in which something meaning is said about something or someone (the subject).

Sujeto – Subject: The person or thing spoken about in a sentence.

Verbo – Verb: A part of speech denoting action or state of being.

Inflexión – Inflection:	Variation in the form of a word to express a variation in function or in meaning.
Forma verbal – Verbal form:	Each one of the words included in the conjugation.
Conjugación – Conjugation:	An orderly and complete list of all the forms of a verb for its moods, tenses, numbers and persons. This term is also used to name the three different classes of Spanish verbs according to the ending of their Inf: Conj 1 for the verbs ending in ar (ganar); Conj 2 for those ending in er (comer); Conj 3 for those ending in ir (vivir).
Modo – Mood:	The form of the verb which denotes the style or manner of the action. There are three moods: indicativo, imperativo, subjuntivo.
Indicativo – Indicative:	The mood of assertion or fact: yo leo, I read.
Imperativo – Imperative:	The mood of command: lee, read.
Subjuntivo – Subjunctive:	The mood of doubt or suppositon, wish, contingency or the like; dudo que ya haya venido, I doubt he has already come.
Formas no personales – Verbals:	The non personal forms of the verb that are employed as nouns, adverbs or adjectives, while still retaining some of the verb functions. There are three verbals: infinitivo, gerundio, participio.

Infinitivo – Infinitive:	The basic form of each verb. It may be substituded by a noun: me gusta <u>cantar</u>; me gustan <u>las canciones</u>; I like <u>to sing</u>, I like <u>songs</u>.
Gerundio – Gerund:	In Spanish it is a verbal adverb. It expresses an action coinciding with the action of the principal verb of the sentence: vi a los niños <u>jugando</u> en el jardín, I saw the children <u>playing</u> in the garden.
Participio – Past Participle:	It is a verbal adjective; cosas <u>vistas</u>, <u>seen</u> things. Mostly used for the compound (perfect) tenses; ya he <u>leído</u> este libro, I have already <u>read</u> this book.
Raíz – Stem:	The first part of each verbal form, consisting of the complete Inf (for Fu and Pos): <u>ganar</u>.-emos, <u>ganar</u>.íamos; or of the Inf less its ending (for all the other tenses): ganar, <u>gan</u>.an, <u>gan</u>.aron, <u>gan</u>. en, etc.
Terminación – Ending:	The second part of each verbal form: ganar. <u>emos</u>, gan.<u>an</u>, ganar.<u>íamos</u>, gan.<u>aron</u>, etc.
Morfema – Morpheme:	The ending is composed of two parts or morphemes: Tem and Pen.
Morfema modo- tiempo – <u>mood</u>- <u>tense</u> morpheme (Pen):	The first part of the ending, which denotes the mood and tense of the form: ganar.<u>e</u> mos, ganar. <u>ía</u> mos, gan.<u>a</u> n, gan.<u>a</u> ron, etc.
Morfema número- persona – <u>N</u>umber-<u>person</u> morpheme (Pen):	The second part of the ending, which denotes the number and person of the form: ganar.e <u>mos</u>, ganar.ía <u>mos</u>, gan.a <u>n</u>, gan.a <u>ron</u>, etc.

Paradigma –   A model of conjugation, giving a list of verbal
Paradigm: forms.

A Complete Conjugation

A complete conjugation is the set of all the inflections of a verb, giving the forms for its moods, tenses, persons and numbers. For each simple tense there is a compound (perfect) tense formed by the corresponding simple tense of the auxiliary verb haber plus the past participle (masculine singular) of the verb being conjugated: from canto, he cantado; from cantaba, había cantado; etc.

(Conjugation of the auxiliary haber is given on Table 5).

The compound (perfect) tenses are as important and necessary as the simple tenses. But for forming the perfect tenses of all the Spanish verbs it is only needed to know how the auxiliary haber is conjugated. Therefore it is absolutely superfluous to spend paper and time in each of the paradigms of Conj 1, Conj 2 and Conj 3, as done in almost all Spanish grammars, since the endings of all persons of all verbs (regular and irregular) are shown on TABLE 1 in the plainest and most distinct order.

The following is a list of a complete conjugation. As an example, three persons (Yo, Tu & Els) of each tense are given using the verb cantar (to sing). The names of all tenses are those given by BELLO, with the corresponding English names. Each perfect tense is named by BELLO as the corresponding single tense with the prefix ante: presente, antepresente, pertérito, antepretérito; futuro, antefuturo; etc.

BELLO´s names for the tenses are the only ones employed by most of the grammars and methods published in Spanish America. But as the official names still are those given by the Academia, a correspondence of the BELLO´s names and the ENGLE´s names are given later.

As promised in the Preface, the meaning and usage of each tense (simple and perfect) is given in a special chapter afterwards.

Simple tenses		Compound (perfect) tenses
Presente (pres) – Present	Indicative mood	Antepresente – Present perfect
canto, cantas, cantan		he cantado, has cantado, han cantado
Pretérito (Pas) – Past		Antepretérito – Past perfect
canté, cantaste, cantaron		hube, hubiste, hubieron cantado
Futuro (Fu) – Future		Antefuturo – Future perfect
cantaré, cantarás, cantarán		habré, habrás, habrán cantado
Copretérito (Co) – Imperfect		Antecopretérito – Pluperfect
cantaba, cantabas, cantaban		había, habías, habían cantado
Pospretérito (Pos) – Conditonal		Antecopretérito – Conditional perfect
cantaría, cantarías, cantarían		habría, habrías, habrían cantado
	Imperative mood	
Presente (Imp) – Imperative present		No imperative perfect
canta (Tu), cantad (Vos)		
	Subjunctive mood	
Presente (SuPres) – Present		Antepresente – Present perfect
cante, cantes, canten		haya, hayas, hayan cantado
Pretérito (SuPas) – Past		Antepretérito – Past perfect

cantara, cantaras,		hubiera, hubieras,
cantaran or		hubieran cantado
cantase, cantases,		or hubiese, hubieses,
cantaren		hubiesen cantado
Futuro (SuFu) – Future		Antefuturo – Future perfect
cantare, cantares,		hubiere, hubieres,
cantaren		hubieren cantado
	Verbals	
Infinitivo (Inf) – Infinitive		Infinitivo compuesto – perfect
cantar		haber cantado
Gerundio (Ger) – Gerund		Gerundio compuesto – perfect
cantado		habiendo cantado
Participio (Par) – Past participle		No participle perfect
cantado		

Correspondence of the BELLO's names with the ENGLE's names for all the tenses

Simple tenses		Compound (perfect) tenses	
BELLO	ENGLE	BELLO	ENGLE
	Indicative		
Presente	Same name	Antepresente	Pretérito perfecto compuesto
Pretérito	Pretérito perfecto simple	Antepretérito	Pretérito anterior
Futuro	Same name	Antefuturo	Futuro perfecto
Copretérito	Pretérito imperfecto	Antecopretérito	Pretérito pluscuamperfecto
Pospretérito	Condicional	Antepospretérito	Condicional perfecto
	Imperative		
Presente	Same name	No imperative perfect	

Subjunctive

Presente	Same name	Antepresente	Pretérito perfecto
Pretérito	Pretérito imperfecto	Antepretérito	Pretérito pluscuamperfecto
Futuro	Same name	Antefuturo	Futuro perfecto

Verbals

Infinitivo	Same name	Infinitivo compuesto	Same name
Gerundio	Same name	Gerundio compuesto	Same name
Participio	Same name	No participle perfect	

Usage of Tú and Usted, and of Vosotros and Ustedes

When adressing a single person, Tú is used for talking to children, relatives and close friends. But Usted and not Tú should be used when talking to any other person with whom using the familiar Tú would be impolite. It must be warned that the third person and not the second person is to be used with Usted: Where do you live? --- ¿Dónde vive usted?: vive and not vives.

When speaking with several people, in all Spanish America Ustedes is used as plural for both Tú and Usted. It must be warned also here that the third person and not the second person is to be used with Ustedes: Where do you (plural) live? -- ¿Dónde viven ustedes?: viven and not vivís.

It could seem unnecessary to say anything else about this matter. But I have seen several methods for teaching Spanish to Americans in which the verbal forms corresponding to the second plural person have been eliminated without any explanation. For instance, the present of the verb vivir (to live) is taught this way: yo (I) vivo, tú (familiar singular you) vives, usted (polite singular you) vive, él (he) vive, nosotros (we) vivimos, ustedes (both familiar and polite plural you) viven, ellos (they) viven.

It is undeniable that the only plural of tú vives is now in Spanish America ustedes viven and therefore it would be false and ludicrous to teach that the only correct plural of tú vives should be vosotros vivís. But it is undeniable too that vosotros still is the true plural of tú. And it still is being used so in all of Spain and it is being used so in all the written Spanish printed up to now, except, of course, in writings of current Spanish-Amercian authors.

Therefore, it continues being necessary to teach foreigners the usage of vosotros (the plural second person) as the plural of tú (the singular second person), although warning when and where is now employed.

Meaning and Usage of the Tenses

Indicative Mood

Presente (Pres) – Present. Uses of Pres are the same in Spanish as in English.

For present condition: Este libro tiene 250 páginas (This book has 250 pages).

For habitual action: Diario como a las siete (I dine daily at seven o'clock).

For conditions of all times: La tierra gira alrededor del sol (The earth rotates around the sun).

Historical present: Colón llega a América en 1492 (Columbus arrives in America in 1492).

Instead of the future: Nos vemos a las cinco en mi oficina (We'll see each other in my office at 5 o'clock). El año entrante hay muchos días de fiesta (There will be many holidays next year).

Pretérito (Pas) – Past. As in English it is used for something begun and completed in the past: Ayer comimos pescado (We ate fish yesterday). Los Piratas no jugaron este viernes (The Pirates didn't play this Friday).

Futuro (Fu) – Future. As in English it describes a future action or condition: El tren llegará tarde hoy (the train will arrive late today). Another form for the future is now frequently used in Spanish: ir a (to be going to) plus infinitive: Mañana voy a comer con mi mamá (I am going to dine – I'll dine – with my mother tomorrow).
Fu is also used to express possibility instead of certainty: ¿Qué hora es? (what time is it?). If you are sure, you answer: Son las cinco (It is 5 o'clock). If you are not sure, you may answer: Serán (it might be) las cinco.

Copretérito (Co) – Imperfect: This tense was named by BELLO copretérito (copast) because it is used whenever something has occurred at the same time as another past action: Cuando tú salías yo entraba (when you were leaving I was coming in). Yo leía cuando tú llegaste (I was reading when you arrived).

Note that Co corresponds to the English past pregressive. We can use in Spanish (and frequently use them) all the progressive tenses, but in Spanish they give the idea of a more durable action than the simple forms: Mientras tú estabas durmiendo yo estaba estudiando (while you were sleeping I was studying).

Co is also frequently used when describing the setting is wanted (the background where an action has developed): Los viajeros llegaron en la noche: todo estaba escuro, había muchas nubes, no se veía ninguna estrella (the travelers arrived at night: everything was dark, there were many clouds, no stars could be seen).

Co is also used as a polite way of asking something: ¿Qué deseaba usted? (What did – instead of do – you want?). Yo quería ver unas camisas (I wanted - instead of want – to see some shirts).

Pospretérito (Pos) – Conditional: (In any conditional sentence, the introductory clause is called the protasis; the consequent clause, expressing the result, is called the apodosis.

Pos is generally used as the apodosis of any conditional sentence: Si yo encontrara aquí un buen reloj, lo compraría ahora mismo (If I were to find a good watch here, I would buy it right now).

The name given by BELLO to this tense, pospretérito, means future in the past because it is used this way: Me avisó que vendría (he informed me he would come): informed is a past, the action of coming was, is or will be after the action of informing.

Pos is also used as a more polite way of asking something: Desearía ver unas camisas (I would like to see some shirts): deseo, Pres (I like); deseaba, Co, (I liked) more polite; desearía, Pos, (I would like) still more polite.

Imperative Mood

Imperativo (Imp) – Imperative present. The same uses in English: Ven y escucha (come and listen).

Notice that, in Spanish, only for the positive Tu and Vos there are special forms for the Imp: escucha Tu, escuchad Vos (listen). For the other persons and for the negative the forms of SuPres must be used for the Imp: escuche usted, escuchen ustedes (listen, polite you): comamos temprano hoy (lut us dine early today); no hables (don´t talk).

Subjunctive Mood

Indicative is used for assertions, for certainty. Subjunctive is to be used for doubt, wish, praying, prohibition, etc. In modern English the indicative is now generally used instead of the subjunctive; but in Spanish the subjunctive is mandatory when applicable: Insisto en que leas (never lees) esta carta (I insist that you read this letter).

Presente (SuPres) – Subjunctive present. Espero que vengas mañana (I hope you will come tomorrow). In English, and in some other languages, the future indicative is used in these conditional or temporal sentences. In Spanish the SuPres must be used.

As already said, SuPres forms are to be used for certain cases of imperative or optative sentences: Déjenme en paz (let me alone!); Quiera dios (God grant!).

Pretérito (Su Pas) – Subjunctiv past. In Spanish there are two forms for the SuPas: Si pudiera or pudiese (if I could).

For the protasis of a conditonal sentence, any one of these two forms may be used; but in Mexico the form in –ra is preferred and only in few cases the form in –se is used by some people: Si tuviera or tuviese dinero compraría esta casa (if I had money I would buy this house).

For the apodosis the usual Pos form may almost be substituted by the SuPas form in –ra: Yo querría - Pos - (or quisiera - SuPas -) vivir cerca del mar si pudiera (or pudiste) hacerlo (I would like to live near the sea if I could do so).

Futuro (SuFu) – Subjunctive future. This tense is almost never used verbally, but is generally used in legal texts. It is also called the hypothetical future because it always indicates an eventual possibility: El que lo hiciere será multado (he who ever would did it shall be fined).

Compound (Perfect) Tenses

Indicative Mood

Antepresente – Present perfect. As in English, it indicates an action begun in the past and carried into the present: Yo he vivido en México por muchos años (I have lived in Mexico City for many years). The meaning is that I could still be living there now.

Or it may also indicate an action begun and completed at no specific time: He leído ya este libro (I have already read this book).

Antepretérito – Past Perfect. It indicates an action that has taken place immediately before another past action: Cuando hubo leído la carta, salió (when he had read the letter, he left). In modern Spanish this tense is <u>not</u> in use any more. The <u>simpler</u> Pas is used after <u>tan luego como</u> or a similar phrase: Tan luego como (inmediatamente que) leyó la carta, salió (<u>as soon as</u> he read the letter, he left).

<u>Antefuturo</u> – Future perfect. As in English it describes an action that will occur before another future action: Para cuando regreses, ya <u>habrá oscurecido</u> (By the time you come back, it will have already gotten dark). It is rarely used this way now. It is used, although not frequently anyway, instead of the present perfect to indicate possibility or probability: <u>Habrás sufrido</u> mucho (instead of <u>quizás has</u> sufrido) con tu jaqueca (maybe you have suffered a lot with your headache).

<u>Antecopretérito</u> – Pluperfect. It describes an action that has taken place some time before another past action: Yo ya <u>había leído</u> tu mensaje cuando tú llegaste (I had already read your message when you arrived).

Notice that the pluperfect (<u>había</u> leído) and not the past perfect (<u>hubo</u> leído) is to be used in Spanish to transalte this English past perfect (had read).

<u>Antepospretérito</u> – Conditional perfect. It is used to express a <u>completed</u> action that occurred after a past situation: Esperábamos que ya <u>habría terminado</u> la guerra para cuando el invierno llegase (we hoped that the war would have ended when the winter arrived): the action of ending occurs before the action of arriving, but both were after the action of hoping.

Imperative Mood

There is <u>no</u> imperative perfect.

Subjunctive Mood

<u>Antepresente</u> – Present perfect. It <u>must</u> be used instead of indicative present perfect when used in a sentence of negation, doubt, etc. For an affirmative sentence: Estoy seguro de que ya <u>ha llegado</u> el tren (I am sure that the train has already arrived). For a negative

sentence: No estoy seguro de que ya <u>haya llegado</u> el tren (I am not sure that the train has already arrived).

<u>Antepretérito</u> – Past perfect. It must be used instead of the indicative past perfect when used in a sentence of negation, doubt, etc. For an affirmative sentence: Estaba seguro de que ya <u>había llegado</u> el tren (I was sure that the train had already arrived). For a negative sentence: <u>No</u> estaba seguro de que ya <u>hubiera</u> (or hubiese) llegado el tren (I was not sure that the train had already arrived).

In conditional sentences: Si <u>hubieras venido</u> antes, <u>habrías visto</u> la ardilla (if you had come earlier, you would have seen the squirrel): Notice that for the protasis the forms ending in –ra or in –se are to be used: si <u>hubieras</u> (o <u>hubieses</u>) venido antes; for the apodosis the indicative form ending in –ría is preferably used, although the subjunctive form ending in –ra might also be used, but <u>never</u> the form ending in –se; <u>habrías</u> (or <u>hubieras</u>, but never <u>hubieses</u>) visto la ardilla.

<u>Antefuturo</u> – Future perfect. It describes a completed hypothetical action done. As stated about the SuFu, also this future perfect is never used verbally, and even in legal texts is very rarely used: Si eso <u>hubieren hecho</u>, deberían haber sido castigados (if they would ever done so, they should have been punished).

Composition and use of the <u>single</u> TABLE

As already said in "Definitions", each form of all the simple tenses of a verb is composed of two parts: the stem and the ending. For example, from ganar, gan.amos, ganar.íamos.

The stem consists of the whole Inf (for Fu and Pos): <u>ganar</u>. emos, <u>ganar</u>.íamos; or the Inf less its ending, ganar (for all the other tenses): <u>gan</u>.amos, <u>gan</u>.aban, etc.

The ending is in turn made up of two morphemes: the mood-tense (Tem) morpheme: ganar.<u>e</u> mos, gan.<u>aba</u> n; the number-person (Pen) morpheme: ganar.e <u>mos</u>, gan.aba <u>n</u>.

Verbs are called regular if all their inflections show their stem and their endings according to the general rule. They are called irregular if they modify the stem (or the ending) in certain persons of certain tenses.

But it should be borne in mind that all the irregularities are practically in the stem. The only irregularities in the ending are those pointed at in Note (I) of the TABLE (and the irregularity of "pecularity" denoted as NI: tiñ.ieron).

In the "General List of Irregular Verbs", the kind of irregularity of each verb is marked, and also the tense (or tenses) in which a certain irregularity occurs.

Therefore, knowing the irregularity that the verb being conjugated has, for instance, pensar (to think), a DI verb according to the List, and knowing also through Table 3 which are the only persons in which its stem is modified, the TABLE will be used without any difficulty or inconvenience.

For the accentuation, i.e., for knowing the syllable bearing the stress of each inflection, Spanish is absolutely regular and uniform:

The stress is always borne by the vowel (or diphtong) immeadiately after the stem (taking into account, of course, that for Fu and Pos the stem is the whole Inf): gan.amos, com.ieran, vivir.án. Only exceptions, where the stress is borne by the stem, are Qua Pres (gan.as), Qua SuPres (piens.en), Tu Imp (com.e), Yo and El Pl (pud.e, pud.o), and irregular Par (muer.to).

It might be necessary to state here, in order to avoid misinterpretations, that the separation of the morphemes is exclusively for morphological purposes and does not mean that for the pronunciation, and least at all for spelling, the syllables are to be separated this way. For example, if Nos Pas in the TABLE is shown as com.i.mos, it is by syllables co-mi-mos; if Els SuPas is shown as viv.iera.n it is by syllables vi-vie-ran.

In the chapter "A Few Hints on Pronunciation" the syllabication of Spanish words has been explained.

Distribution of the TABLE is as follows:

Col A is for the persons; Col B for the stem; Col C to Col L for the Tem morpheme corresponding to each of the ten simple tenses. Col M is for the Pen morphemes of all the tenses, except of Pas which uses Col N and of Imp which uses Col O.

The upper half of the TABLE is for verbs of Conj 1 (ganar), the lower half for verbs of Conj 2 and 3 (comer, vivir).

It is <u>obviously</u> realized that by using this SINGLE TABLE it is possible to conjugate a whole verb, or any certain tense, or any odd person.

In each case it is only necessary to add to the stem (regular or irregular) the corresponding Tem morpheme and then the corresponding Pen morpheme: gan.aba.mos, com.i.stes, vivir.e.mos, <u>quis</u>.iera.is, poder.á.n, etc.

T A B L E I

ONE SINGLE TABLE for Conjugation ALL the
Spanish Verbs – Regular and Irregular –
(All the single tenses (1) of the THREE conjugations)

		Mood- Tense (Tem) Morphemes											Number – Person (Pen) Morphemes		
		- Indicative Tenses -						Subjunctive Tenses							
Person	Stem	Pres	Co	Pas	Fu	Pos	Imp	SuPres	SuPas 1	SuPas 2	SuFu	All tenses	Pas	Imp	
(A)	(B)	(C)	(D)	(E)	(F)	(G)	(H)	(I)	(J)	(K)	(L)	(M)	(N)	(O)
Yo	Gan	o	aba	é	é	ía		e	ara	ase	are	-	-	
Tu	Gan	a	aba	a	á	ía	a	e	ara	ase	are	s	stes	s
El	Gan	a	aba	a	á	ía		e	ara	ase	are	-	ó	
Nos	Gan	a	ába	a	e	ía		e	ára	áre	áre	mos	mos	
Vos	Gan	a	aba	a	é	ía	a	e	ara	are	are	is	ste is	d
Els	Gan	a	aba	a	á	ía		e	ara	áre	áre	n	ron	
Yo	Com	o	ía	í	é	ía		a	iera	iese	iere	-	-	
Tu	Viv	e	ía	i	á	ía	e	a	iera	iese	iere	s	stes	s
El	Com	e	ía	i	á	ía		a	iera	iese	iere	-	ó	
Nos	Viv	e.i	ía	i	e	ía		a	iéra	iése	iére	mos	mos	
Vos	Com	é.i	ía	i	é	ía	e.i	a	iera	iese	iere	is	ste is	d
Els	Viv	e	ía	ie	á	ía		a	iera	iese	iére	n	ron	
		(3)			(2)	(2)	(3)						(4)	(4)	(4)

Conj 1 (ar) — rows with Gan stem
Conj 2/3 (er.ir) — rows with Com/Viv stem

Verbals

	Infinitive (Inf)	Gerund (Ger)	Participle (Par)	
Conj 1	Gan ar	Gan ando	Gan ado	Conj 1
Conj 2/3	Com/Viv er.ir	Com/Viv iendo	Com/Viv ido	Conj 2/3

(1)   Only excepetions: Yo and El Pl (tuve instead of tení), shortened
Tu Imp (ten instead of tien.e), some persons of the Pres of

haber and ser (has instead of hab.es, son instead of s.en);
irregular Par (muerto instead of mor.ido).

(2)   The stem for Fu and Pos is the whole Inf, either the regular
        Inf (ganar) or the irregular Inf (saber, decir). In bygone Spanish
        these forms were two separate words. Morirás (you will die)
        was morir has (to die you have). That is why the endings,
        including the Tem morpheme, are the same for the three
        conjugations.

(3)   Remember that only three forms (Nos Pres, Vos Pres and Vos
        Imp) have a difference in the Tem morpheme between Conj 2
        and Conj 3. That is why this Tem morpheme is shown in the
        TABLE as e.i (com.e.mos, viv.i.mos).

(4)   Notice that for each person the Pen morphemes are the same
        for the three conjugations and are the same for all the tenses
        with the only exceptions of four persons of the Pas and the
        two persons of the Imp.

Remember that a diagonal line over a letter means that this
letter must be omitted. In this TABLE s as Pen morpheme is
put instead of (-) just to point out that the s, which is the Pen
morpheme of Tu in all tenses, must be omitted in Tu Pas and
Tu Imp. It must always be said ganaste, never ganastes.

T A B L E I

(modified to make certain special points stand out)

The modification from the orginial TABLE has been:

The tenses are now arranged horizontally – by lines – not by columns

The persons are now arranged vertically – by columns – not by lines

Stem	Tense	Yo Morphemes Tem I	2/3	Pen	Tu Morphemes Tem I	2/3	Pen	El Morphemes Tem I	2/3	Pen	Nos Morphemes Tem I	2/3	Pen	Vos Morphemes Tem I	2/3	Pen	Els Morphemes Tem I	2/3	Pen
	Conj ...	I	2/3		I	2/3		I	2/3		I	2/3		I	2/3		I	2/3	
1	Pres	o	o	_	a	e	s	a	e.i	-	a	e.i	mos	á	é.i	is	a	e	n
ganar	Co	aba	ía	-	aba	ía	s	ába	ía	-	ába	ía	mos	aba	ía	is	aba	ía	n
	Pas	é	í	_	a	i	stes	a	i	ó	a	i	mos	a	i	ste is	a	ie	ron
2	SuPres	e	a	_	e	a	s	e	a	-	e	a	mos	é	á	is	e	a	n
comer	SuPas 1	ara	iera	_	ara	iera	s	ára	iéra	-	ára	iéra	mos	ara	iera	is	ara	iera	n
	SuPas 2	ase	iese	_	ase	iese	s	áse	iése	-	áse	iése	mos	ase	iese	is	ase	iese	n
3	SuFu			_	are	iere	s	áre	iére	-	áre	iére	mos	are	iere	is	are	iere	n
vivir	Imp				a	e	s							a	e.i	d			
	Conj...	1/2/3		_	1/2/3			1/2/3			1/2/3			1/2/3			1/2/3		
ganar	Fu	é		_	á		s	á		-	e		mos	é		is	á		n
comer																			
vivir	Pos	ía		_	ía		s	ía		-	ía		mos	ía		is	ía		n

In the original TABLE it stands out that the Tem morphemes, although _different_ for each tense, are _the_ same for the corresponding _six_ persons with very few exceptions.

In this modified table it continues being obvious that the Tem morphemes are different for each tense; but it is also _more visible_ the difference that exists between the Tem morphemes of the verbs of Conj 1 and those of the verbs of Conj 2/3.

In this modified table it is also <u>more visible</u> that the Pen morphemes are, for each person, <u>exactly the same</u> for the <u>three</u> conjugations and for <u>all</u> the tenses, with the <u>only</u> exceptions of four persons of the Pas and the two persons of the Imp.

Maybe some readers will find easier the use of this modified table. Anyway, with the original TABLE of this one a whole verb, any tense or any odd person can be conjugated without difficulty. The only thing to do is to add to the stem (regualr or irregular) of the verb, first the Tem morpheme and then the Pen morpheme.

It always must be remembered that table 3 makes known which are the <u>only</u> persons affected by each irregularity.

Drills for getting acquainted with the TABLE
Whole tenses

Past (Pas) of the regualr verb <u>temer</u>:
It is of Conj 2, the lower part of the TABLE is used. For stem, the
Inf less its ending. For Tem morpheme,
Col. E. For Pen morpheme, Col N.

Yo	temer	í	-	temí
Tu	tem	i	stes	temiste
El	tem	i	ó	temió
Nos	tem	i	mos	temimos
Vos	tem	i	steis	tesmisteis
Els	tem	ie	ron	temieron

Future (Fu) of the regular verb <u>sumir</u>:
For Fu, either the upper or the lower part of the TABLE is
used. For stem, the whole Inf. For Tem
morpheme, Col F. For Pen morpheme, Col. M.

Yo	sumir	é	-	sumiré
Tu	sumir	á	s	sumirás
El	sumir	á	-	sumirá
Nos	sumir	e	mos	sumiremos
Vos	sumir	é	is	sumiréis
Els	sumir	á	n	sumirán

Present, subjunctive (SuPres) of the irregular DI verb <u>quebrar</u>.
It is of Conj 1, the upper part of the TABLE is used. For stem,
the Inf less its ending; according to
Table 3 Qua Pres change from quebr to quiebr. For Tem
morpheme, Col. I. For Pen
morpheme, Col M.

Yo	qui<u>e</u>br	e	-	quiebre
Tu	qui<u>e</u>br	e	s	quiebres
El	qui<u>e</u>br	e	-	quiebre

Nos	quebr	e	mos	quebremos
Vos	quebr	é	is	quebreis
Els	quiebr	e	n	quiebren

Odd Persons

Regular verbs

Verb	Person & tense	Stem	Tem Col	Pen Col	Stem	Tem	Pen	
prestar	Yo SuPres	prest	I	M	prest	e	-	preste
correr	Nos SuPres	corr	J	M	corr	iéra	mos	corriéramos
toser	Els Pas	tos	E	N	tos	ie	ron	tosieron
pulir	Tu Imp	pul	H	O	pul	e	s	pule
hablar	Vos Fu	hablar	F	M	hablar	é	is	hablaréis

Irregular verbs

Verb	Class	Person & tense	Stem	Tem Col	Pen Col	Stem	Tem	Pen	
temblar	DI	Tu Pres	tiembl	C	M	tiembl	a	s	tiemblas
estar	MO	Els Co	est	D	M	est	aba	n	estaban R
pedir	VO	Els Pas	pid	E	N	pid	ie	ron	pidieron
crecer	GU	Tu Imp	crec	H	O	crec	e	s	crece R
huir	YE	Vos SuPres	huy	I	M	huy	á	is	huyáis
crecer	GU	Yo Pres	crezc	C	M	crezc	o	-	crezco
tener	PI	Vos Pas	tuv	E	N	tuv	i	steis	tuvisteis
traer	GU	Els Fu	traer	F	M	traer	á	n	traerán R
gruñir	NI	Els SuPas	gruñ	J	M	gruñ	ie	ron	gruñieron

PART TWO

A Separate Study of Each Irregularity

Introduction

In order to make the learning of the Spanish verbs easy and simple, the only logical way is to study the irregularities separately, after having classified them in a minimum of groups.

The present work is based on this consideration: To study in first place the four irregularities of the present tense, then the three irregularities of the past and the irregularity of the future.

Of the many reasons existing to support this method, those presented in the following paragraphs are more than enough.

ENGLE, BELLO and many other grammarians have decided that the irregularities of the past participle are so few that they can be treated "later on", i.e., separately.

Now, according to ENGLE the irregular past participles (abierto, etc.) are 17, the irregular PI pasts (anduve, etc.) are only 16, the irregular FI futures (cabré, etc.) are only 12.

Then, if PI pasts and the FI futures are so few and are less in number than the irregular past participles, the only logical thing is to also leave their study for a later occasion, i.e., to study them separately too.

BELLO says it insistently and ENGLE ratifies it: Spanish conjugation is very regular, even in its irregularities. All grammarians point out that all the irregularities, with very few exceptions, are in the stem. But it is not generally pointed out that absolutely all the irregular verbs (except andar) have some kind of irregularity in the present, and about 90 per cent are irregular in the present tense only.

If of the six groups or irregularities made by BELLO to include all the irregular verbs, four affect the present, and PI and FI (the other two) comprise so few single verbs, it becomes logical to study these two separately.

23

ENGLE, BELLO and many other grammarians teach that a variation (an irregularity) appearing in a certain tense appears also in certain other tense or tenses. That is, tenses are divided into (as I have called them) original and imitating tenses. But it is not pointed out insistently that an imitating tense imitates unavoidably and unbreakably one original tense.

It must be specially remarked that the irregularity of an original tense never appears in any other person or tense, but exclusively in certain persons of the corresponding imitating tenses.

To make this stand out, Table 2 shows in a most clear way which of the ten single tenses are original, which are imitating and which are independent.

Table 3, in turn, teaches exactly which are the only persons affected by each irregularity.

Thus, it is confirmed that Pres, Pas and Fu are the three original tenses and each one of these three has its own and exclusive imitating tenses. They form three completely different groups. The logical and convenient move is, then, to study separately each irregularity.

BELLO and ENGLE report that two irregularities happen to concur within some verbs. They teach that this concurring is subject to a strict rule according to which one of the two modified stems must be preferred in the imitating tenses. For instance, oír (to hear) which in the Pres is GU oigo and YE oyes, in the SuPres, its imitating tense, obeys to the GU stem (oiga, oigas, etc.) and not to the YE stem (oya, oyas, etc.). But what must be taken into account is that the two irregularities must occur in the same tense. A minor though very important point is that this concurring happens only in the present and only in four cases. That is why these four cases will be treated in this paper separately and specially in the final chapter of the "Irregularities in the Present".

It should not be said that an irregularity in the Pres concurs with another irregularity which appears in the Pas, or in the Fu, or in both. For instance, the three irregularities of the verb hacer, hago in the Pres, hice in the Pas, and haré in the Fu are completely independent from each other.

It is possible and convenient to study each one separately, as its irregular Par <u>hecho</u> is studied separately too.

It is true that the VO irregularity affects always <u>two</u> original tenses, the Pres and the Pas. But Table 3 demonstrates that each of these original tenses has its own and exclusive imitating tenses. That is why it becomes convenient to study the VO irregularity separately, first with the other Pres irregularities and later with the other Pas irregularities.

Some grammarians come near my idea of studying separately the different irregularities; but no one decides to do so because, as one of them says, the greatest difficulty consists in that <u>not a few</u> verbs have more than one irregularity.

ENGLE, for example, says that it happens <u>with some frequency</u> that two of more irregularities of different classes appear within the same verb. Table 4 shows that <u>very few</u>, only <u>ten</u>, are the <u>simple</u> verbs associating a PI and a FI to an irregularity in the Pres.

It is of course necessary and convenient to know, after having studied the irregularities separately, which verbs have associated several of them. Table 4, which occupies only <u>half a page</u>, groups and lists <u>all</u> the simple verbs showing more than one irregularity.

Finally, many methods for teaching languages study exclusively the present of the verbs in the first lessons (ten or more). Among ourselves, if a child (or a foreigner) says <u>no sabo</u> (I don´t know), he is told to say <u>no sé</u>. But he is not explained in that moment that the verb saber has more than one associated irregularity, that <u>supe</u> must be said instead of <u>sabí</u>, and <u>sabré</u> instead of <u>saberé</u>. All these teachings are left for more a timely occasion.

We are going, then, to study each class of irregularity separately, following the order given in Table 3. When studying, for instance, the GU verbs, we will not be preoccupied at all with whether one of these verbs has or does not have any associated irregularities, as grammarians never are preoccupied with whether one of these verbs has or does not have an irregular participle.

Another warning is: Sometimes, to avoid unnecessary long lists, only the simple verbs will be listed. Compound verbs have <u>always</u> the <u>same</u> irregularities as the corresponding simple verb, save very few exceptions which will be opportunely pointed out. It is, therefore, implied that <u>com</u>poner, <u>dis</u>poner, <u>ex</u>poner, <u>im</u>poner, etc., have the same irregularities as <u>poner</u> (to put).

The following order will always be obeyed for the study of each irregularity:

a)   The features defining this irregularity
b)   The <u>only</u> persons affected by this irregularity
c)   The list of verbs which have this irregularity.

N.B. ENGLE, BELLO and many grammars and methods list among the Spanish irregular verbs some ones like alebrarse, apernar, desflocar, dolar, enhestar, etc., which are never heard nor read in Mexico. Therefore I have omitted them from my lists.

T A B L E   2

Original Tenses and Imitating Tenses

	In the present	In the past	In the future
Original tense	Pres	Pas	Fu
Imitating tense	SuPres	SuPas 1 & 2	Pos
Imitating tense	Tu Imp	SuFu	
Imitating tense		Ger	
Independent tense	Co	Always regular (only exceptions: era, iba, veía)	
Independent tense	Vos Imp	Always regular (without exception)	
Independent tense	Par	Almost always regular (few exceptions: roto, muerto, impreso, hecho, etc.)	

T A B L E   3

Only persons Affected by Each Irregularity

Original tenses				Imitating tenses			
Of the present							
	GU	-	Yo Pres	Seis	SuPres		
	DI	-	Qua Pres	Qua	SuPres	Tu	Imp
	VO	-	Qua Pres	Seis	SuPres	Tu	Imp
	YE	-	Qua Pres	Seis	SuPres	Tu	Imp
Of the past							
	PI	-	Seis Pas	Seis	SuPas 1&2	Seis SuFu	
	VO	-	El & Els Pas	Seis	SuPas 1&2	Seis SuFu	Ger

NI	-	El & Els Pas	Seis	SuPas 1&2	Seis SuFu	Ger
Of the future						
FI	-	Seis Fu	Seis Pos			

N.B. Some PI and VO forms may be NI too. But because PI and VO irregularities affect the <u>stem</u> and NI affects the <u>ending</u> they cannot disturb each other (For example: PI and NI, dij.ieron; VO and NI, riñ.ió).

Table 2 shows very distinctly which of <u>all</u> the simple tenses are, in the irregular verbs, the <u>original</u> tenses; which one are the <u>imitating</u> tenses; which ones are the <u>independent</u> tenses.

Table 3, on the other hand, shows which ones are the <u>only</u> persons affected by each irregularity.

With these two tables it is plainly demonstrated that the original tenses are <u>three</u>: Pres, Pas and Fu; that each one of the three groups which are formed holds its <u>own</u> exclusive and inescapable imitating tenses; that each imitating tense <u>does</u> inescapably and unbreakably imitate a certain, and <u>never</u> any other, original tense. This demonstrates that the irregularities of the Spanish verbs are subject to very strict rules.

The logical and convenient move is, then, to study each irregularity <u>separately</u>.

Illustrative Examples for Table 3
(They may serve as a paradigm for ANY irregular verb)

(The affected persons have been underlined)

	GU	DI	VO	YE		PI	VO	NI		FI
	crec.er	rod.ar	ped.ir	hu.ir		pon.er	ped.ir	tañ.er		haber
	Pres	Pres	Pres	Pres		Pas	Pas	Pas		Fu
Yo	crezc.o	rued.o	pid.o	huy.o	Yo	pus.e	pedí	tañí	Yo	habr.é
Tu	creces	ruedas	pides	huyes	Tu	pusiste	pediste	tañiste	Tu	habrás
El	crece	rueda	pide	huye	El	puso	pid.ió	tañ.ió	El	habrá
Nos	crecemos	rodamos	pedimos	huimos	Nos	pusimos	pedimos	tañimos	Nos	habremos
Vos	crecéis	rodáis	pedís	huís	Vos	pusisteis	pedisteis	teñisteis	Vos	habréis
Els	crecen	ruedan	piden	huyen	Els	pusieron	pidieron	tañieron	Els	habrán

	SuPres	SuPres	SuPres	SuPres		SuPas I	SuPas I	SuPas I		Pos
Yo	crezca	ruede	pida	huya	Yo	pusiera	pidiera	tañiera	Yo	habría
Tu	crezcas	ruedes	pidas	huyas	Tu	pusieras	pidieras	tañieras	Tu	habrías
El	crezca	ruede	pida	huya	El	pusiera	pidiera	tañiera	El	habría
Nos	crezcamos	rodemos	pidamos	huyamos	Nos	pusiéramos	pidiéramos	tañiéramos	Nos	habríamos
Vos	crezcáis	rodéis	pidáis	huyáis	Vos	pusierais	pidierais	tañierais	Vos	habríais
Els	cerzcan	rueden	pidan	huyan	Els	pusieran	pidieran	tañieran	Els	habrían

	Imp	Imp	Imp	Imp		SuPas 2	SuPas 2	SuPas 2
Tu	crece (*)	rueda	pide	huye	Yo	pusiese	pidiese	tañiese
					Tu	pusieses	pidieses	tañieses
					etc.	etc.	etc.	etc.

		SuFu	SuFu	SuFu
	Yo	pusiere	pidiere	tañiere
	Tu	pusieres	pidieres	tañieres
	etc.	etc.	etc.	etc.

	Ger	Ger	Ger
	pon.iendo (*)	pid.iendo	tañ.iendo

As shown by Table 3

(*) Tu Imp <u>does not</u> imitate GU. It is crec.e, not crez.que

(*) Ger does not imitate PI. It is pon.iendo, not pus.iendo

Changes in Spelling

A simple change in spelling does not constitute an irregularity: A letter must be substituted by another one whenever it is necessary for avoiding the alteration of the original sound. According to the present Spanish spelling rules, the following series of letters require such a change:

ca	que	qui	co	cu	--	K sound (English cat quay)
ga	gue	gui	go	gu	--	GG sound (English gap, guest)
za	ce	ci	zo	zu	--	SS sound (English ceiling)
ja	ge	gi	jo	ju	--	H sound (English hand)
gua	güe	güi	guo		--	GWA sound: use or omission of (¨) diaeresis

These changes are necessary and occur throughout Spanish words: For plurals of nouns and adjectives, for augmentatives and diminutives, for all kinds of derivatives: lápiz, lápices; feroz, feroces; toca, toquilla; vaca, vaquero; cirugía, cirujano; paraguas, paragüería; etc.

The changes must be applied, of course, to the verbal inflections too. The general rule for the verbs is: The same letter that the stem has in the Inf must be kept throughout the conjugation: from pecar, peco, pecaba, pecaste, pecarás, etc. But the change in letter is mandatory in order for Inf sound not to change: pequé, pequemos, etc.; because otherwise pecé, pecemos would be pronounced pessé, pessemos, instead of peké, pekemos. That is why, for instance, from rogar, rogué, and not rogé must be written; from exigir, exijo and not exigo; etc.

Using as usual my abbreviations, there is an easiest and practical way of knowing which persons are those requiring such a change:

For verbs of Conj I (in ar)

	Yo Pas		Seis SuPres			
Pecar	pequé	peque	peques	pequemos	pequéis	pequen
Apagar	apagué	apague	apagues	apaguemos	apaguéis	apaguen
Fraguar	fragüé	fragüe	fragües	fragüemos	fragüéis	fragüen

For verbs of Conj 2/3 (in er/ir)

	Yo Pres		Seis SuPres			
Escoger	escojo	escoja	escojas	escojamos	escojáis	escojan
Delinquir	delinco	delinca	delincas	delincamos	delincáis	delincan
Zurcir	zurzo	zurzas	zurzas	zurzamos	zurzáis	zurzan

Verbs with an Inf ending in <u>aer</u>, <u>eer</u>, <u>oer</u>, <u>oir</u> and <u>uir</u> are not irregular either when they change the <u>i</u> of their ending into a <u>y</u>. Because when this <u>i</u> comes to be the beginning of a syllable (from caer, ca-ió), it acquires when being pronounced a consonant sound (ca-<u>yó</u>). It requires therefore a consonant in the spelling. The persons where this change occurs, without being irregular, are:

	El & Els Pas	Seis SuPas 1	Seis SuPas 2	Seis SuFu	Ger
Caer	cayó, cayeron	cayera, etc.	cayese, etc.	cayere, etc.	cayendo
Leer	leyó, leyeron	leyera, etc.	leyese, etc.	leyere, etc.	leyendo
Oír	oyó, oyeron	oyera, etc.	oyese, etc.	oyere, etc.	oyendo

On the other hand, all YE verbs (their Inf ends in <u>uir</u>) are positively irregular in the following persons:

	Qua Pres	Seis SuPres	Tu Imp
Huir	huyo huyes huye	huya huyas huyamos	huye
	huyen	huyáis huyan	

because in these persons the <u>y</u> is <u>added</u> to the stem: hu.ir, huy.o instead of hú.o.

In "Irregularities in the Past", the NI irregularity will be studied in detail. It consists of <u>taking out</u> from the pronunciation, and therefore from the spelling, the i of the ending of certain persons: bull.ió, traj. iera, ri.iendo, etc.

Irregularities in the Present

GU Irregularity

The feature defining this irregularity is: A guttural sound (k or g) appears in the stem, which was not in the Inf: cono<u>c</u>er, cono<u>zc</u>o and not conozo; valer, val<u>g</u>o and not valo; caer, ca<u>i</u>go and not cao; hacer, hago and not hazo, etc.

The <u>only</u> affected persons, as shown by Table 3, are <u>always</u>:

Yo Pres   Seis SuPres

The verbs having this irregularity are:

All verbs ending in acer, ecer, ocer, ucir change <u>c</u> into <u>zc</u>: nacer, nazco, crecer, crezco; conocer, conozco; lucir, luzco. As there are in the Academia's dictionary more than 200 verbs ending in <u>ecer</u>, all the verbs more in use will be included in the "General List of Irregular Verbs", but only a few of them will be given, as examples, in the following list. As verbs ending in <u>acer</u>, <u>ocer</u> and <u>ucir</u> are so few, also the compound verbs will be included now in the list.

nacer	amanecer	obedecer	conocer	aducir
renacer	aparecer	oscurecer	desconocer	conducir
pacer	crecer	permanecer	reconocer	deducir
placer	enloquecer	pertenecer		inducir
complacer	entristecer	rejuvenecer	lucir	introducir
yacer	envejecer	resplandecer	deslucir	producir
fallecer	reverdecer	enlucir	reducir	
aborrecer	favorecer	robustecer	relucir	seducir
agradecer	merecer		traducir	

Only exceptions are: <u>Hacer</u> is GU, but its YO Pres is hago and not ha<u>zc</u>o. <u>Mecer</u> is now generally used as regualr, mezo, although several grammarians say that me<u>zc</u>o is still correct too. Cocer is DI and not GU: its correct Yo Pres is c<u>ue</u>zo and it is used so by many people; but city people in Mexico prefer to improperly use it as a regular verb: co<u>zo</u>.

These other <u>six</u> simple verbs put a gg sound to the Inf:

caer,	caigo,	caiga	hacer, hago, haga	poner, pongo, ponga
treaer,	traigo,	traiga	valer, valgo, valga	salir, salgo, salga

The following <u>four</u> verbs are GU too; but as they have another concurring irregularity in the present, they will be studied in the chapter "Verbs with a double irregularity in the present":

tener	it is GU and DI	Pres:	GU Yo tengo,	DI Tu t<u>ie</u>nes
venir	it is GU and DI	Pres:	GU Yo vengo,	Di Tu v<u>ie</u>nes
decir	it is GU and VO	Pres:	GU Yo digo,	VO Tu d<u>i</u>ces
oír	it is GU and YE	Pres:	Gu Yo oigo,	VO Tu o<u>y</u>es

There are <u>three</u> additional GU verbs, but they are rarely used in Mexico:

asir	asgo	asga.	Only the <u>asir</u> and <u>asido</u> forms are occasionally used.
raer	raigo	raiga.	Only <u>raer</u> and <u>raído</u> are occasionally used.
roer	roigo	roiga.	Never used. The regular roo, roa, is sometimes used by city people; royo, roya is used by peasants.

Finally, the <u>three</u> following verbs are included by several grammarians among the GU verbs (as I am doing here), because the only affected persons in the present are precisely <u>Yo Pres</u> and <u>Seis SuPres</u>, which is the characteristic of the GU irregularity. They are:

caber, quepo, quepa	saber, sepo, sepa	ver, veo, vea

Irregularites in the Present

DI Irregularity

The feature defining this irregularity is: A vowel of the stem is turned into a diptong: <u>e</u> changes into <u>ie</u> (c<u>e</u>gar, c<u>ie</u>go); o changes into ue (moler, muelo). In the only two verbs, i changes into ie (adquirir, adquiero); in only one verb, u changes into ue (jugar, juego).

The only persons affected, as shown by Table 3, are always:

Qua Pres   Qua SuPres   Tu Imp

Verbs with this irregularity are numerous. It is the only one in Spanish for which there is no practical rule for indicating which verbs undergo the diphtongation. Most DI verbs belong to Conj 1.

A curious condition is that verbs of Conj 1 do not posses any other irregularity whatsoever but the DI irregularity in the present. By exception, three verbs of Conj 1, andar, dar and estar are PI, which is an irregularity in the past.

As it has already been said, only the simple verbs will be given in the following lists, to avoid unnecessary long lists.

Verbs that change e into ie:

Conj 1

acertar	calentar	despertar	escarmentar	negar	segar
acrecentar	cegar	emparentar	estregar	nevar	sembrar
alentar	cerrar	empedrar	fregar	pensar (1)	sentar
apacentar	comentar	empezar	gobernar	plegar	presentar (R)
apretar	comenzar	encomendar	helar	quebrar	sosegar
arrendar	concertar	enmendar	herrar	recomendar	temblar
aserrar	confesar	ensangrentar	incesar	regar	tentar (2)
atravesar	profesar (R)	enterrar	manifestar	remendar	trasegar
aventar	derrengar	errar (yerro)	mentar (3)	reventar	tropezar
	desmembrar		merendar		

Conj 2

(a)scender	defender	encender	perder	tender	tener (4)
cerner(se)	ofender (R)	heder	querer	pretender (R)	verter

Conj 3

concernir   discernir   hendir   hervir (4)   erguir (4)   venir (4)

Verbs that change o into ue:

Conj 1

acordar	colar	degollar	forzar	regoldar	soltar
acostar	colgar	denostar	holgar	renovar	sonar
almorzar	concordar	desaforar	hollar	innovar (R)	soñar
amolar	consolar	descollar	mostrar	resollar	tostar
apostar	contar	desollar	poblar	rodar	trocar
asolar	cornar	encordar	probar	rogar (5)	tronar
avergonzar	costar	encontrar	recordar	soldar	volar
		engrosar			volcar

Conj 2

cocer	llover	morder	oler (huelo)	soler	torcer
doler	moler	mover	poder	(ab)solver	volver

Conj 3

dormir (4)   morir (4)

Verbs that change i into ie:

adquirir   inquirir

Verb that changes u into ue:

Conj 1

jugar

(1)   All other verbs ending in ensar, as compensar, etc., are R.
(2)   All other verbs ending in tentar, as atentar, contentar, etc. are R.

(3)   All other verbs ending in mentar, as comentar, lamentar, etc., are R.

(4)   The verbs cernir, hervir, erguir, and those ending in entir, arir and ertir, (also dormir and morir) are DI and VO in the present (muera, muramos).
Tener and venir are DI overlapped by GU (tengo, tienes). Both cases will be specially studied in the chapter "Verbs with a double irregularity in the present".

(5)   All other verbs ending in rogar, as derogar, prorrogar, etc. are R.

There is a tendency to diphthongize the stem of some DI verbs in the Inf making them regular throughout this way: amueblar instead of the original amoblar. The grammarians consider this acceptable. So, amueblar, deshielar, deshierbar, deshuesar, empuercar, encuerar, encluecar, angruesar, anmielar, entiesar, and maybe some others, are now in general use in Mexico. ENGLE lists them, of course, as DI: amoblar, deshelar, etc.

The other tendency, which is considered reproachable, incorrect, unlearnead, is to conjugate some DI verbs as regular, i.e., not diphthongized in the present: se renova instead of se renueva. In Mexico, hardly anybody diphthongizes now asolar, forzar, renovar, soldar, desoldar, trocar. And it is more and more frequent to hear concertar, acrecentar, nevar, and maybe some other verbs as regular. Quebrar, querer and maybe some other verbs are improperly conjugated as regular by peasants only.

I have mentioned before that in Mexico the city people improperly use (from cocer) cozo instead of cuezo. On the other hand, almost everybody incorrectly diphtongizes templar and destemplar, and there are even some people who diphthongize sorber too.

Irregularities in the present

VO irregularity

(It has been already pointed out that the VO irregularity affects the present and also the past. But, as shown by Tables 2 and 3, the imitating tenses of Pres are completely different from the imitating tenses of Pas. It is advantageous, therefore, to study this VO irregularity in the present separately now, and leave the study of the VO irregularity in the past for a later chapter.)

The feature defining this irregularity is: The e of the stem is changed into i: from pedir, pido. For dormir and morir the o is changed into u: durmamos, muramos.

The only persos affected, as shown by Table 3, are always:

Qua Pres   Seis SuPres   Tu Imp

Verbs with this irregularity are: All verbs of Conj 3 that have an e as the vowel of the last (or only) syllable of their stem: embestir, pedir, gemir, etc.

As they are relatively few, the following list includes both the simple and the compound verbs:

ceñir	elegir	gemir	impedir	reñir	teñir
desceñir	colegir	henchir	expedir	seguir	desteñir
competir	reelegir	medir	reexpedir	conseguir	reteñir
repetir	embestir	desmedir(se)	reír	perseguir	vestir
concebir	engreír(se)	comedir(se)	sonreír	proseguir	desvestir
constreñir	freír	descomedir(se)	regir	servir	investir
estreñir	refreír	pedir	corregir	derretir	revestir
desleír	sofreír	despedir	rendir		travestir

Cernir, erguir, hervir, and all verbs ending in entir, erir and ertir are of course VO verbs too; but as VO is overlapped by DI in the present (sentir, siento, sintamos), they will be studied later in the chapter "Verbs with a double irregularity in the present". These other (simple and compund) VO verbs are:

advertir	subvertir	referir	erguir	mentir	sentir
controvertir	conferir	transferir	herir	desmentir	asentir

convertir	deferir	adherir	malherir	requerir	consentir
divertir	diferir	arrepentir(se)	zaherir	sugerir	disentir
invertir	inferir	cernir	hervir		presentir
pervertir	preferir	digerir	rehervir		resentir
revertir	proferir	ingerir	injerir		

The only exceptions are:
Sumergir, convergir and divergir are regular.
Agredir and transgredir are not defective verbs in Mexico. They are conjugated as R.
Concernir, discernir and hendir are DI, not VO (concierne, discierne, hienda).

Dormir and morir are VO verbs too; but as VO is overlapped by DI in the present (dormir, duermo, durmamos), they will be studied later in the mentioned chapter too.

Pudrir is totally regular, except that its Par is always podrido and never pudrido, and that it has two correct Inf: podrir, pudrir.

Irregularities in the present

YE irregularity

The feature defining this irregularity is: A y is added to the stem: from hu.ir, huy.o, huy.amos instead of hú.o, hu.amos.

The only persons affected, as shown by Table 3, are always:

Qua Pres   Seis SuPres   Tu Imp

Verbs with this irregularity are: All verbs ending in uir. As they are a few, the following list includes both simple and the compound verbs:

argüir	circuir	estatuir	construir	disminiuir	huir
redargüir	concluir	constituir	destruir	fluir	rehuir

atribuir	excluir	destituir	instruir	afluir	imbuir
contribuir	incluir	instituir	obstruir	confluir	inmiscuir
distribuir	recluir	prostituir	reconstruir	influir	intuir
retribuir		restituir	derruir	refluir	luir
		sustituir			diluir

Oír is a YE verb too; but as YE is overlapped by GU in the present (oir, oigo, oyes), it will be studied later in the chapter "Verbs with a double irregularity in the present".

Remember what was said under "Changes in spelling":

YE verbs, which end in uir, should not be considered as irregular because they change i into y in the endings of El and Els Pas, Seis SuPas 1 & 2, Seis SuFu and Ger: from hu.ir, hu.yó instead of hu.ió, hu.yendo instead of hu.iendo, etc.

But they are truely irregular in Qua Pres, Seis SuPres and Tu Imp because a y is added to the stem: huy.o instead of hú.o, etc.

Irregularities in the present

Verbs with a double Irregularity in the Present

BELLO gives a good rule (248): If a verb has two irregularities, one of the stem is to be preferred over the other, being the preference to be given in the order GU, DI, VO, YE, i.e., the GU stem must be preferred over the DI, the VO, or the YE stem; the DI stem must be preferred over the VO stem.

But this rule needs two explanations:

a) The concurrence of the two irregularities must be in the same tense;

b) The predominating irregularity will be imitated by its own imitating persons only.

If these explanations are taken into account and use is made of Table 3 for determining which are the only persons affected by the predominating irregularity, it is easy to solve the only <u>four cases</u> of Spanish single verbs having two irregularities in the <u>same</u> tense: in the <u>present</u>.

First case: DI overlapped by GU

There are only <u>two</u> simple verbs: tener and venir: GU Yo Pres tengo, vengo; DI Tu Pres tienes, vienes.

According to BELLO´s rule, GU predominates over DI in the imitating tenses.

According to Table 3:	imitating tense of GU is	Seis SuPres
imitating tenses of DI are	Qua SuPres	Tu Imp

Therefore, the GU irregularity tengo is imitated by Seis SuPres, tenga, tengas, etc., instead of tiena, tienas, etc. So, the DI irregularity is completely eliminated in the SuPres.

But Tu Imp is <u>not</u> imitating a GU irregularity: it cannot be tengue, vengue; it should continue to be DI, tiene, viene. In this particular case it is not so because the Tu Imp of tener and venir happen to be apocopated (shortened) forms: ten, ven (See Irregularities of the Tu Imp).

Second case: VO overlapped by GU

There is <u>only</u> one simple verb: decir, GU Yo Pres <u>digo</u>, Vo Tu Pres dices.

According to BELLO´s rule, GU predominates over VO in the imitating tense.

According to Table 3:	imitating tense of GU is Seis	Su Pres
imitating tenses of VO are Seis		Su Pres Tu Imp

Therefore, the GU irregularity digo is imitated by Seis SuPres diga, digas, etc. So, the VO irregularity is completely eliminated in the SuPres.

But Tu Imp is <u>not</u> imitating a GU irregularity: it cannot be digue; it should continue to be VO, dice. In this particular case it is not so because the Tu Imp of decir happens to be an apocopated form di.

But in the compund verbs of decir, bendecir, predecir, etc., Tu Imp <u>does</u> remain VO: ben<u>dice</u>, pre<u>dice</u>, etc.

Third case: YE overlapped by GU

There is only one simple verb: oír: GU Yo Pres oigo, YE Tu Pres oyes. According to BELLO's rule, GU predominates over YE in the imitating tense.

According to Table 3:	imitating tense of GU is	Seis SuPres imitating tenses of YE are	Seis SuPres	Tu Imp

Therefore, the GU irregularity oigo is imitated by Seis SuPres oiga, oigas, etc., instead of oya, oyas, etc. So, the YE irregularity is completely eliminated in the SuPres.

But Tu Imp is not imitating a GU irregularity: it cannot be oigue; it should remain to be YE, it is oye.

Fourth case: VO overlapped by DI

The verbs affected by this double irregularity in the present are: cernir, erguir, hervir, and those ending in entir, erir and ertir: in the SuPres hierva, hirvamos.

The complete list of the simple and compund verbs affected by this double irregularity is the second list of the chapter Irregularities in the present – VO irregularity.

Dormir and morir are also included in this fourth case (duerma, durmamos; muera, muramos).

According to BELLO's rule, DI predominates over VO in the imitating tenses.

According to Table 3,	DI tenses are	Qua Pres	Qua SuPres	Tu Imp
	VO tenses are	Qua Pres	Seis SuPres	Tu Imp

In the Pres and Tu Imp the VO irregularity is completely eliminated:

DI	Qua Pres	hiervo, hierves, hierve, hierven	Tu Imp	hierve

VO	Qua Pres	hirvo, hirves, hirve, hirven	Tu Imp	hirve
DI	Qua Pres	muero, mueres, muere, mueren	Tu Imp	muere
VO	Qua Pres	muro, mures, mure, muren	Tu Imp	mure

But in the SuPres, Qua SuPres and not Seis SuPres are the imitating persons of the predominating DI irregularity. For this reason the VO Nos and Vos SuPres persons were not eliminated, they do remain being VO:

DI	Qua SuPres	hierva, hiervas, hierva,	hiervan
VO	Seis SuPres	hirva, hirvas, hirva, hirvamos, hirváis,	hirvan

DI	Qua SuPres	duerma, duermas, duerma,	duerman
VO	Seis SuPres	durma, durmas, durma, durmamos, durmáis,	durman

The great advantage and usefullness of Table 3 is shown here: the only persons affected for each irregularity are exaclty determined. It is proved again that the irregulairties of the Spanish verbs are subject to very strict rules. The hybrid SuPres of the verbs of this fourth case becomes perfectly justified, explained and clarified:

hierva   hiervas   hierva   --   hirvamos hirváis   --   hiervan

duerma duermas duerma -- durmamos durmáis -- duerman

Irregularities in the Past

PI irregularity

The features defining this irregularity are:

The stem undergoes some vowel and consonant changes: cab. er, cup.e, cup.iste, etc.

The stress, in Yo and El Pas, is borne by the stem and not by the ending as it occurs on all the other verbs: cupe, cupo, instead of cupí, cupió.

The endings of the Pas of all PI verbs are those corresponding to Conj 2/3, although and<u>ar</u>, est<u>ar</u> and d<u>ar</u> are verbs of Conj 1: andu. vi<u>ste</u> instead of anduv.<u>aste</u>, estuv.<u>imos</u> instead of estuv.<u>amos</u>; d.<u>ieron</u> instead of d.<u>aron</u>.

The <u>only</u> persons affected, as shown in Table 3, are <u>always</u>:

| Seis Pas | Seis SuPas 1 | Seis SuPas 2 | Seis SuFu |

There are <u>only</u> <u>fourteen</u> simple verbs having this irregularity:

Conj 1	and.ar	anduv.e	anduv.o	estuv.ieron	
	est.ar	estuv.e	estuv.o	estuv.ieron	(it is a MO verb)
Conj 2	cab.er	cup.e	cup.o	cup.ieron	
	hab.er	hub.e	hub.o	hub.ieron	(it is a MO verb)
	hac.er	hic.e	hiz.o	hic.ieron	
	pod.er	pud.e	pud.o	pud.ieron	
	pon.er	pus.e	pus.o	pus.ieron	
	quer.er	quis.e	quis.o	quis.ieron	
	sab.er	sup.e	sup.o	sup.ieron	
	ten.er	tuv.e	tuv.o	tuv.ieron	
	tra.er	traj.e	traj.o	traj.ieron NI	
Conj 3	dec.ir	dij.e	dij.o	dij.ieron NI	
	duc.ir	induj.e	induj.o	induj.ieron NI	(the simple ducir is not used)
	ven.ir	vin.e	vin.o	vin.ieron	

ENGLE includes among the PI verbs other two which are obsolete and not used in Mexico:

plac.er	plug.o	
respond.er	repus.e	repus.o

All six MO verbs <u>do</u> posses a PI Pas. ENBLE says (2.12.9) wholly in the right that in some of them the PI irregularity is hidden due to their one-syllable form. Then, they must be included here:

d.ar	d.i	d.io	d.ieron
s.er	fu.i	fu.e	fu.ieron
v.er	v.i	v.io	v.ieron
ir	f.ui	fu.e	fu.ieron

<u>Andar</u>: This verb is the <u>only</u> exception to a very general rule: A Spanish verb is <u>surely</u> regular if its Yo Pres is regular. Andar is a PI verb (anduve) although its Yo Pres (ando) is regular.

<u>Venir</u>: Many educated people in Mexico still use, in the Pas of this verb, the regular forms v<u>e</u>niste, v<u>e</u>nimos, v<u>e</u>nisteis, which are considered by all grammarians, if not definitely incorrect, definitely obsolete. In <u>all</u> PI verbs, the irregularity of the <u>six</u> persons of their Pas is <u>uniform</u>: The <u>only</u> correct forms, then, are vine, v<u>i</u>niste, v<u>i</u>nimos, v<u>i</u>nisteis, vinieron.

<u>Ver</u>: Our peasants still use for Yo and El Pas of the verb ver the obsolete forms v<u>i</u>de, v<u>i</u>do, instead of the modern correct forms v<u>i</u>, v<u>i</u>o. A similar thing happens to the verb <u>traer</u>: our peasants still use obsolete forms for the Pas: tr<u>u</u>je, tr<u>u</u>jiste, tr<u>u</u>jo, etc., instead of the modern correct forms, tr<u>a</u>je, tr<u>a</u>jiste, tr<u>a</u>jo, etc.

Notice that, as indicated by Table 3, Ger IS NOT an imitator of Els Pas in the PI verbs: from <u>est</u>.ar, estuv.ieron, the Ger is not estuv.iendo but <u>est</u>.ando; from d.ar, d.ieron, the Ger is not d.iendo but d.<u>ando</u>; from <u>quer</u>.er, quis.ieron, the Ger is <u>quer</u>.iendo and not quis.iendo.

Irregularites in the Past

<u>VO irregularity</u>

The feature defining this irregularity is: An <u>e</u> of the stem is changed into <u>i</u>: p<u>e</u>dir, p<u>i</u>dió. D<u>o</u>rmir and m<u>o</u>rir change the <u>o</u> into <u>u</u>: d<u>u</u>rmió, m<u>u</u>rieron.

The <u>only</u> persons affected, as shown by Table 3, are <u>always</u>:

El and Els Pas   Seis SuPas 1   Seis SuPas 2   Seis SuFu   Ger

Verbs with this irregularity are:

All those verbs of Conj 3 that have an e as the vowel of the last (or only) syllable of their stem: emb<u>e</u>stir, p<u>e</u>dir, etc. As it can be seen, they are <u>exactly</u> the same which have the VO irregularity in the present.

And of course, cernir, erguir, hervir, and all the verbs ending in entir, erir and ertir (that in the Pres are VO, but overlapped by DI) are to be included here because in the Pas they are simply VO without any complication. Both lists were given when studying the VO irregularity in the present.

The advantage (or it could be said the necessity) of studying this VO irregularity in the past separately from the VO irregularity in the present is seen and felt evident here. In the past there is never a concurrence of the two irregularities VI and DI because DI is an irregularity exclusively of the present (as shown by Tables 2 and 3) and it can never concur with an irregularity of the past.

The only exceptions, as pointed out when studying the VO irregularity in the present, are:

Sumergir, convergir, divergir, and in Mexico agredir and transgredir, are R.
Concernir, discernir and hendir, which in the Pres are only DI, are of course regular in the Pas.

Decir and venir should be VO because they end in ir and have an e as the vowel of the stem. But they are PI in the past, so consequently their El Pas is <u>dijo</u> and <u>vino</u> instead of <u>dició</u> and <u>vinió</u>.

Dormir and morir, although VO overlapped by DI in the present, in the past are simply VO without any complication.

Verbs ending in eír and eñir (r<u>e</u>ír, r<u>e</u>ñir, etc.) are in the past VO and NI, but these two irregularities, as explained in Table 3, never affect each other (r<u>i</u>.ieron, r<u>i</u>ñ.ieron).

Irregularities in the Past

NI irregularity

The feature defining this irregularity is: The i of the ending of El and Els Pas (and its imitating tenses) is omitted: bull.ió, bull.iera, bull. iendo, etc.

The <u>only</u> persons affected, as shown by Table 3, are <u>always</u>:

El and Els Pas   Seis SuPas I   Seis SuPas 2   Seis SuFu   Ger

Verbs eith this irregularity may be classified in three groups:

1) – All verbs ending in llir, ñer and ñir, both regular and irregular: bullir, bull.ió, tañer, tañ.ieron; gruñir, gruñ.iera; t<u>e</u>ñir, t<u>i</u>ñ.iendo, etc. No grammarian wants to call the omission of the i in these cases an irregularity. BELLO says it is a necessary suppression as it becomes difficult, if not impossible, to pronounce this i. ENGLE says an <u>i</u> is already immersed in the ll or the ñ.

For the verb henchir (so stuff), some grammarians say the i must be omitted (hinch.io) because it is as difficult and cacophonic to pronounce this i after the ch as after the ll or the ñ. But other grammarians say it must be pronounced to distinguish hinch.ió of henchir from hinch.ó of hinchar (to swell). In Mexico we pronounce the i after ch in several words: Chietla, Chiapas, achiote, etc.

2) – All verbs ending in eír (r<u>e</u>ír, fr<u>e</u>ír) which are also VO verbs (r<u>i</u>.ió, fr<u>i</u>.ió). ENGLE says this is a true irregularity, although BELLO calls it an "accident". It is obvious anyway that the present froms ri.ó, fri.era are more euphonic (harmonious) than riyó, friyeran.

3)   – The three verbs decir, ducir, traer (and of course their compounds: bendecir, conducir, atraer, etc.). Their Els Pas (dij.ieron, conduj.ieron, etc.) and their imitating tenses (dij.iera, conduj.ieses, etc.) omit the i̲ too. BELLO says it is a "pecularity", although he admits that in all other verbs ending in ger, gir, jer and jir the i̲ is never omitted (recoger, recogió; fingir, fingiera; tejer, tejieron; crujir, crujiendo; etc.)

Many people forget the peculiarity of those three verbs decir, ducir, traer, and improperly pronounce bendijieron, condujiese, atrajiera, etc.

The Els Pas of the verbs ser and ir and their imitating tenses (fueron, fuéramos, etc.) are the only other cases in the Spanish conjugation where the i̲ of the ending is omitted. That is why they have been included by me as NI verbs just to point out his "peculiarity".

Irregularities in the Future

FI irregularity

The feature defining this irregularity is: The complete Inf (which serves as stem for Fu and Pos) is syncopated (shortened) in some verbs: podr.é instead of poder.é, tendr.é instead of tener.é, dir.é instead of decir.é, etc.

The only persons affected, as shown by Table 3, are always:

Sies Fu   Seis Pos

There are only twelve simple verbs having this irregularity: In five cases the vowel of the stem disappears: habr instead of haber. In other five cases, in addition of losing the vowel, a d̲ is interposed:

pon**d**r instead of poner. In the other two cases, two letters disappear: dir instead of d**ec**ir, har instead of ha**ce**r.

caber	cabr.é	instead of	cab**er**.é
haber	habr.é	instead of	hab**er**.é
poder	podr.é	instead of	pod**er**.é
querer	querr.é	instead of	quer**er**.é
saber	sabr.é	instead of	sab**er**.é
poner	pon**d**r.é	instead of	pon**er**.é
tener	ten**d**r.é	instead of	ten**er**.é
valer	val**d**r.é	instead of	val**er**.é
salir	sal**d**r.é	instead of	sal**ir**.é
venir	ven**d**r.é	instead of	ven**ir**.é
hacer	har.é	instead of	ha**ce**r.é
decir	dir.é	instead of	dec**ir**.é

Of que**re**r, many people improperly say que**dr**é instead of que**rr**é. May be it is more euphonic, but the only correct Fu is que**rr**é.

Of satisfacer, a compound of hacer, several grammarians judge (and I have the same opinion) that satisfa**ce**ré (the regular Fu) sounds much better than satisfaré.

Of bendecir and maldecir, all grammarians are in agreement in stating that their current correct Fu is bend**ec**iré and mald**ec**iré (the regular Fu).

But of contradecir, desdecir and predecir, the most used compounds of decir, several grammarians judge (and I have the same opinion) that contra**dec**iré, des**dec**iré and pre**dec**iré, the regular Fu, sounds much better; although other grammarians say that contradiré, desdiré and prediré, following the simple diré, are the only orthodox Fu of these verbs.

Irregularities of the Tu Imp

As shown by TABLE 1, the Tu forms of all the tenses have an s as Pen morpheme (ganas, comías, vivirás, hubieras, etc.) except Tu Pas and Tu Imp (ganastes, comes).

As shown by Table 3, Tu Imp is a faithful imitator of Qua Pres of the DI, VO and YE verbs: Di negar, niego, Tu Imp niega; Vo pedir, pides, Tu Imp pide; YE huir, huyen, Tu Imp huye. But it is not an imitator of Yo Pres of the GU verbs: atraer, atraigo, Tu Imp atrae.

A general rule for the Tu Imp of all verbs (both regular and irregular) can then be given: The form Tu Imp is the same as the form Tu Pres omitting the final s: ganar, ganas – gana; negar, niegas – niega; pedir, pides – pide; etc.

Only six simple verbs do not follow this rule, because they have an apocopated (shortened) Tu Imp:

decir: di instead of dice, hacer: haz instead of hace; poner, pon instead of pone; salir: sal instead of sale; tener: ten instead of tiene; venir: ven instead of viene.

Some compound verbs do not imitate the shortened Tu Imp of their simple verbs: they have a complete Tu Imp:

From bendecir: bendice, maldice, contradice, desdice, predice.
From hacer: satisface.
From salir: sobresale.

Three MO verbs (haber, ser and ir) do not obey this rule either, because their Tu Pres are very irregular (has, eres, vas). Their Tu Imp are: hé, sé, vé.

In Mexico the Tu Imp of oír is sometimes familiarly shortened: oy instead of oye: "Oy lo que están diciendo de tí" (hear what is being said about you).

Irregularities of the Gerund

As shown by Table 3, Ger is a constant imitator of El and Els Pas of the VO and the NI verbs. But Ger is not an imitator of Six Pas of the PI verbs.

A general rule can then be given: Ger imitates only the VO and the NI irregularities. Ger is regular in any other Spanish verb, including the PI verbs.

Examples:	Inf	Els Pas	Ger
A regular verb	ganar	gan.aron	gan.ando
A regular verb	comer	com.ieron	com.iendo
A regular verb	vivir	viv.ieron	viv.iendo
A PI verb	estar	estuv.ieron	est.ando R
A PI verb	hacer	hic.ieron	hac.iendo R
A VO verb	pedir	pid.ieron	pid.iendo VO
A VO verb	morir	mur.ieron	mur.iendo VO
A NI verb	tañer	tañ.ieron	tañ.iendo NI
A VO & NI verb	teñir	tiñ.ieron	tiñ.iendo VO & NI

Decir and venir are verbs of Conj 3 and their stem vowel is an e: they are therefore VO verbs (overlapped by PI). They must continue obeying the rule: their Ger must imitate the VO irregularity: their Ger must be and is diciendo, viniendo.

The verb poder, although of Conj 2, exceptionally happens to be a VO verb in the past like dormir and morir (durmieron, murieron, pudieron). Although it is in the past overlapped by PI (pude, pudo), its Ger must be and is VO: pudiendo.

A curious coincidence: in venir and poder the VO and PI irregularities coincide in Els Pas: vin.ieron, pud.ieron.

Irregularities in the past participle

As a general rule, Par is <u>regular</u> in Spanish. It is one of the outstanding examples of the extraordinary regularity of the Spanish conjugation. <u>No</u> other existing language has so few irregular past participles as Spanish.

As shown by Table 2, Par is totally <u>independent</u>. It does <u>not</u> imitate any original irregular tense.

The irregularities of Par are:

Changes in some letters of the stem: <u>pon</u>.er, <u>pues</u>.to.

The ending is <u>cho</u>, <u>so</u> or <u>to</u> instead of ido: muer.<u>to</u> instead of mori.do.

The stress is on the stem and not on the ending; ' <u>vuel</u>. to, not volv.'<u>i</u>do.

There are <u>only</u> <u>twelve</u> irregular Par. And a curious fact is that <u>five</u> of them, alomst half of the total, are perfectly regular verbs in all the rest of their conjugation. Maybe that is why all grammarians have agreed to treat the irregularities of the Par separately.

The five verbs, entirely regular in the rest of their conjugations, are:

abrir	-	and its compound verbs:	abierto	- entreabierto, etc.
cubrir	-	and its compound verbs:	cubierto	- descubierto, encubierto, etc.
(e)scribir	-	and its compound verbs:	escrito	- descrito, inscrito, etc.
(im)primir		<u>not</u> its compound verbs:	impreso	- comprimido, deprimido, etc.
romper	-	<u>not</u> its compound verb:	roto	- corrompido

The other seven verbs are:

decir	-	not its compound verbs:	dicho	-	bendecido, (maldito), contradicho, etc.
(ab)solver	-	and its compound verbs:	absuelto	-	disuelto, resuelto, etc.
hacer	-	and its compound verbs:	hecho	-	deshecho, satisfecho, etc.
morir	-	and its compound verbs:	muerto	-	
poner	-	and its compound verbs:	puesto	-	compuesto, dispuesto, etc.
ver	-	and its compound verbs:	visto	-	previsto, etc.
volver	-	and its compound verbs:	vuelto	-	devuelto, envuelto, etc.

There are, according to ENGLE and other grammarians, several verbs which have two past participles, one regular and the other irregular. What concerning them is practiced in Mexico is the following:

imprimir - the regular imprimido is sometimes used for the perfect tenses: no han imprimido todavía mi libro; or when used as synonym of to impart: le han imprimido más velocidad.

romper - the regular rompido is used only by children and unlearned people.

proveer - the regular proveído is used only by courts and other government offices. In the usual meaning of supplied, provisto is always used.

freír - the regular freído may always be used for the compound tenses: no has freído el pollo. For the result frito must be used: estos huevos no están bien fritos.

matar   -   the regular matado is always used. Muerto is <u>never</u> used
                    as a Part of matar as in Spain: me han <u>muerto</u> a mi hijo
                    (my son has been killed).

prender   -   the regular prendido is always used. Preso is never used
                    as Part; prender is never used with the meaning <u>to</u>
                    <u>arrest</u>.

Of bendecir and maldecir, compound verbs of decir, everybody agrees that the regular past participle must be used for their perfect tenses. And that a special past participle (bendito, maldito) is used as adjective and for passive phrases: bendito seas (be blessed).

But of contradecir, desdecir and predecir, other usual compound verbs of decir, many grammarians judge (and it is my opinion too) that the regular participle sounds much better. I prefer "a mí nadie me ha contradecido ni desdecido nunca" rahter than "a mí nadie me ha contradicho ni desdicho nunca".

A warning: Many grammars and dictionaries still teach that there are other verbs with two past participles, one regular and the other irregular (for example, comprimido and compreso). But it is not true: the irregular ones may <u>never</u> be used as past participle: they are mere adjectives.

T A B L E 4

Verbs with MORE THAN ONE irregularity

Verb	Pres	SuPres	El & Els Pas	Fu	Imp	Co
oír	GU oigo YE oyes etc.	GU oiga oigas	R	R		
herir	DI hiero (I)	DI hiera VO hiramos	VO hirieron	R		
morir	DI muero (I)	DI muera VO muramos	VO murieron	R		
caber	GU quepo	GU quepa	PI cupieron	FI cabré		
saber	GU sépo	GU sepa	PI supieron	FI sabré		
hacer	GU hago	GU haga	PI hicieron	FI haré	haz	
poner	GU pongo	GU ponga	PI pusieron	FI pondré	pon	
tener	GU tengo DI tienes	GU tenga	PI tuvieron	FI tendré	ten	
venir	GU vengo DI vienes	GU venga	PI vinieron	FI vendré	ven	
decir	GU digo VO dices	CU diga	PI dijieron NI	FI diré	di	
ducir	GU (re)duzco	GU reduzca	PI redujieron NI	R		
traer	GU traigo	GU traiga	PI trajieron NI	R		
poder	DI puedo	DI pueda	PI pudieron	FI podré		
querer	DI quiero	DI quiera	PI quisieron	FI querré		
valer	GU valgo	GU valga	R	FI valdré	val *	
salir	GU salgo	GU salga	R	FI saldré	sal	
reír	VO río	VO ría	VO riieron NI	R		
teñir	VO tiño	VO riña	VO tiñieron NI	R		
		MO verbs				
dar	MO doy das da etc.	MO des dé den etc.	PI dieron	R		
estar	MO estoy estás etc.	MO esté estés etc.	PI estuvieron	R		
haber	MO he has ha etc.	MO haya hayas etc.	PI hubieron	FI habré	hé	
ir	MO voy vas va etc.	MO vaya vayas etc.	PI fuieron MO NI	R	vé	MO iba

| ser | MO soy eres es etc. | MO sea seas sea etc. | PI fuieron MO NI | R | | MO era |
| ver | GU veo ves ve etc. | GU vea veas vea etc. | PI vido * vieron | R | | MO veía |

(1) Verbs with VO overlapped by DI are: cernir, erguir, hervir, and those ending in entir, erir and ertir (sentir, herir, adveritr, etc.). Also dormir and morir.

*   The forms marked with an asterisk * are obsolete.

This Table 4, taking up a little more than a score of lines, groups ALL the simple verbs which have MORE THAN ONE irregularity. It proves that the irregularities in the past or in the future are independent of those in the present. It cannot be said that they imitate or obey each other: for instance, from the verb caber, quepo, cupe, cabré.

This table demonstrates the tremendous regularity of the Spanish conjugation; it makes evident the fact that all difficulties and complications disappear if each irregularity is studied separately.

Peculiar irregularities of the MO Verbs

As stated in the "List of Abbreviations" six Spanish verbs have such particular irregularities in their conjugation as to be worthy of a special treatment. All grammarians have done so. To study them I have grouped them under the name of MO (monosyllabic) verbs. They are:

dar   estar   haber   ser   ver   ir

Some readers will say that neither estar nor haber are monosyllabic.

Estar is indeed so: It behaves entirley as if it were star. The initial e is false. It has been added just because there cannot be any word beginning with a liquid s in Spanish. Even English words used by Spanish speaking people are pronounced esport, esmog, estándar, etc.

Haber has a Pres as monosyllabic as the other MO verbs: he, has, ha, han.

Two MO verbs, ser and ir, (like the English to be and to go), are the only ones in Spanish having not one but several stems:

From ser: Co: ér.amos   Pas: fu.imos   Fu: ser.emos
From ir: Pres: v.amos   Pas: fu.imos   Fu: ir.emos

In Table 5 the six MO verbs are conjugated. What Note (I) of TABLE I expresses is corroborated here: The Tem morphemes are the same as those of all other Spanish verbs, except some persons of the Pres of haber and ser.

In the following lines the pecularities of the MO verbs will be described, tense by tense, following the order of Table 2 (the original and their corresponding imitating tenses).

In the Pres:

The very pecularity of all the MO verbs, as noticed by all grammarians, is the stress. In all other Spanish verbs, in Qua Pres, Qua

SuPres and Tu Imp, the stress is borne, not by the ending but by the stem: cant.o, dig.as, com.e. This becomes impossible for the MO verbs: Being monosyllabic forms, the stress has to be borne by the ending: has, ves, den, estén.

All Spanish verbs (regular and irregular) make their Yo Pres by adding just an o to the stem: gan.ar, gan.o; mor.ir, muer.o; etc.

The Yo Pres of four MO verbs (the only really monosyllabic Yo Pres forms) add a euphonic y to the final o: d.oy, est.oy, s.oy, v.oy.

Only one MO verb, haber, has a shortened Yo Pres: he, hebo. It shares this pecularity with just another Spanish verb, saber: its Yo Pres is sé, sepo.

All Spanish verbs (regular and irregular) have standard endings for their Pres. Only the MO verbs haber and ser have special forms:

Haber:	It is:	he	has	ha		hemos	habéis	han
If R it would be:		habo	habes	habe	habemos	habéis	haben	

Ser:	It is:	soy	eres	es		somos	sois	son
If R it would be:		so	ses	se	semos	seis	sen	

The endings of the Pres of ir would be as regular as those of dar and estar if its real Inf were var instead of ir: v.oy, v.as, v.a, v.amos, v.ais, v.an.

In the SuPres

In all Spanish verbs (regular and irregular), SuPres uses the same stem of the corresponding Yo Pres: comer: com.o, com.a, comas, etc; tener: teng.o, teng.a, teng.as, etc; quebrar: quiebro, quiebre, quiebres, etc.

Three MO verbs are the only exceptions:

Haber:	Stem for Yo Pres: h.e	Stem for the SuPres:	hay.a, hay.as, etc.

Ser:	Stem for Yo	Stem for the	se.a, se.as,
	Pres: s.oy	SuPres:	etc.
Ir:	Stem for Yo	Stem for the	vay.a, vay.
	Pres: v.oy	SuPres:	as, etc.

In the Past:

An almost incredible point: The forms of the Past (and imitating tenses) for ser (to be) are the same as for ir (to go):

Yo fui, tú fuiste, él fue, etc. (I was, you were, he was, etc.)
Yo fui, tú fuiste, él fue, etc. (I went, you went, he went, etc.)

As pointed out so soundly by ENGLE (2.12.9), the reduction to monosyllabic forms of their Yo and El Pas hides the PI nature of the MO verbs dar, ser, ver and ir: All six MO verbs must be included, as I did when studying the PI irregularity, among the other PI verbs.

Of the verbs ser and ir, the endings of their Yo and El Pas are different form those of all the other Spanish verbs: A regular verb: com. er, com.í, com.ió; a PI verb: hab.er, hub.e, hub.o; ser or ir, fui, fue.

Of the verbs ser and ir: When studying the NI irregularity it was already remarked that their Els Pas fu.eron is a very special exception of the general ending ieron of all Els Pas of the verbs of Conj 2/3.

Of ver: The obsolete forms vide, vido, instead of the present forms Yo vi, El vio, are still used in Mexico by the peasants.
Of dar: The present forms Yo di, El dio, probably were many years ago something like Yo dide, El Dido, as those of the verb ver.

In the Fu:

Haber is the only MO verb with an irregular Fu: habré instead of haber.é.

In the Tu Imp:

Only ir, among the MO verbs, has a really irregular Tu Imp: v.é, because the stem v. is irregular. (See the chapter "Irregularities of the Tu Imp").

Ir is the only verb in Spanish having a special form for the optative Nos: it is more frequently said vamos rather than vayamos to mean let us go.

For the purpose of avoiding a confusion between vé (see) from ver and vé (go) from ir, in Mexico vé (go) is often subsituted with anda from the verb andar (to walk, to go): Anda a ver quién llegó (go to see who came). Sometimes it even is duplicated: Anda vé a comprar unos dulces (go go to buy some candies).

In the Co:

Co is always regular in Spanish verbs: gan.aba, quebr.aba, com. ía, parec.ía, ped.ía, hu.ía, hab.ía, d.aba, etc.

The only exceptions are the irregular Co of the two MO verbs:

| From ser: | era | eras | era | éramos | erais | eran |
| From ir: | iba | ibas | iba | íbamos | ibais | iban |

From ver: The Co veía, veías, etc. (instead of vía, vías, etc.) is not considered as a truely irregular Co: It is just the regular Co of the obsolete Inf veer (instead of ver).

In the Par:

Only ver, among the MO verbs, has an irregular Par: visto instead of v.ido.

The compound verbs of ver, for instance, prever (to forsee), through a very special exception, keep the stress on the endings of Tu, El and Els Pres, and Tu Imp, even if they are not monosyllabic forms any more: Tu prevés, El prevé, Els prevén, prevé Tu.

T A B L E 5

Conjugation of the MO verbs

(following the order of Table 2: original tenses
and their corresponding imitating tenses)

	Dar	Estar	Haber	Ser	Ver	Ir
	Pres	Pres	Pres	Pres	Pres	Pres
Yo	d o y	est o y	h e (bo)	s o y	ve o -	v o y
Tu	d a s	est á s	h a s	er e s	v e s	v a s
El	d a -	est á -	h a -	es - -	v e -	v a -
Nos	d a mos	est a mos	h e mos	s o mos	v e mos	v a mos
Vos	d a is	est á is	hab é is	s o is	v e is	v a is
Els	d a n	est á n	h a n	s o n	v e n	v a n
	SuPres	SuPres	SuPres	SuPres	SuPres	SuPres
Yo	d é -	est é -	hay a -	se a -	ve a -	vay a -
Tu	d e s	est é s	hay a s	se a s	ve a s	vay a s
etc.	etc.	etc.	etc.	etc.	etc.	etc.
	Tu Imp	Tu Imp	Tu Imp	Tu Imp	Tu Imp	Tu Imp
Tu	d a -	est á -	h é -	s é -	v é -	v é -
	Pas	Pas	Pas	Pas	Pas	Pas
Yo	d i -	estuv – e	hub – e	fu i -	v i -	fu i -
Tu	d i ste	estuv i ste	hub i ste	fu i ste	v i ste	fu i ste
El	d i o	estuv – o	hub – o	fu – e	v i o	fu – e
Nos	d i mos	estuv i mos	hub i mos	fu i mos	v i mos	fu i mos
Vos	d i steis	estuv i steis	hub i steis	fu i steis	v i steis	fu i steis
Els	d ie ron	estuv ie ron	hub ie ron	fu ie ron	v ie ron	fu ie ron
	SuPas & SuFu	SuPas & SuFu	SuPas & SuFu	SuPas & SuFu	SuPas & SuFu	SuPas & SuFu
Yo	d iera -	estuv iera -	hub iera -	fu iera -	v iera -	fu iera -
Tu	d iese s	estuv iese s	hub iese s	fu eses s	v iese s	fu ese s
El	d iere -	estuv iere -	hub iere -	fu ere -	v iere -	fu ere -
etc.	etc.	etc.	etc.	etc.	etc.	etc.
	Fu	Fu	Fu	Fu	Fu	Fu
Yo	dar é -	estar é -	habr é -	ser é -	ver é -	ir é -

Tu	dar á s	estar á s	habr á s	ser á s	ver á s	ir á s
etc.	etc.	etc.	etc.	etc.	etc.	etc.
	Pos	Pos	Pos	Pos	Pos	Pos
Yo	dar ía -	estar ía -	habr ía -	ser ía -	ver ía -	ir ía -
Tu	dar ía s	estar ía s	habr ía s	ser ía s	ver ía s	ir ía s
etc.	etc.	etc.	etc.	etc.	etc.	etc.
	Co	Co	Co	Co	Co	Co
Yo	d aba -	est aba -	hab ía -	er a -	ve ía -	- iba -
Tu	d aba s	est aba s	hab ía s	er a s	ve ía s	- iba s
El	d aba -	est aba -	hab ía -	er a-	ve ía -	- iba -
Nos	d ába mos	est ába mos	hab ía mos	ér a mos	ve ía mos	- íba mos
Vos	d aba is	est aba is	hab ía is	er a is	ve ía is	- iba is
Els	d aba n	est aba n	hab ía n	er a n	ve ía n	- iba n
	Ger	Ger	Ger	Ger	Ger	Ger
	d a ndo	est a ndo	hab ie ndo	s ie ndo	v ie ndo	- ye ndo
	Par	Par	Par	Par	Par	Par
	d a do	est a do	hab i do	s i do	vis - to	- i do

Verbs ending in iar and uar

All vebs ending in iar (as confiar and copiar) and in uar (as acentuar and averiguar) are regular. Presumably that is why most grammarians do not take the trouble of studying them in spite of offering the problem of the stress in their Qua Pres, Qua SuPres and Tu Imp which bear the stress on the stem and not on the ending. Some of these verbs bear the stress on the i or the u (con' fí-o, acen'tú-o) dissolving the diphtong; others bear the stress on the previous syllable (' co-pio, ave' ri-guo) keeping the diphtong.

Those ending in iar

Most of them bear the stress on the previuos syllable ('co-pio, a'gra-vio, reve'ren-cio, 'lim-pio, etc.) keeping thus the diphtong. As it can be said that the majority do so, it is unnecessary to list them.

The following list includes, then, the simple and compound verbs that bear the stress on the i dissolving the diphtong (con'fí-o, 'guí-o, des'ví-o, etc.).

criar	guiar	enfriar	estirar	esquiar	ataviar
fiar	liar	resfriar	fotografiar	extasiar(se)	contrariar
confiar	aliar	expiar	and all	arriar	variar
porfiar	desliar	amnistiar	those	descarriar	desvariar
desafiar	desviar	averiar	ending	chirriar	ampliar
desconfiar	enviar	espiar	in	rociar	inventariar
piar	extraviar	hastiar	grafiar		

Of the verbs ending in iar that ENGLE indicates there is no doubt among the speakers on which syllable the stress falls, the more general pronunciation in Mexio is: se 'a-graia, se a'fi-lia, se ca'rí-an (the teeth), con'ci-lia, recon'ci-lia, au'xi-lia, an'sí-a, re'pa-tria, se glo'-ría, se va'cí-a, se vana'glo-ria, se 'vi-dria.

Those ending in uar

The general rule is: If the verb ends in cuar or guar the diphtong is kept: apro'pin-cuo, ave'ri-guo. But if the consonant before the u is any other than c or g the diphtong is dissolved: acen'tú-o, conti'nú-o, insi'nú-o, va' lú-o, etc.

Although very few verbs and in cuar, for some of them there is doubt as to how they should be pronounced. In Mexico it is more often heard eva'cú-o than e'va-cuo, and ade'cú-o than a'de-cuo, and li'cú-o than 'li-cuo; but more often pro'mis-cuo than promis'cú-o.

Defective verbs

Grammarians call defective a verb lacking one of more forms. According to this definition there is no defective verb in Spanish. All verbs theoretically could be conjugated totally. But of course some forms will never be used.

Some forms are not used for their odd sound: abuelo from abolir, etc. Some forms may turn out to be impossible or absurd: BELLO says poder (to be able to) does not lend itself to the imperative. Many verbs are used only in their Par: despavorido, etc.

Some verbs, which are called impersonal, admit only one person: the singular third person: llueve (it rains), mañana nevará (it will snow tomorrow). But it is not so because the other persons are lacking. They can be used in figurative language: llovieron golpes (there rained blows).

Other verbs are only used in the two third persons: esto no te atañe (this does not concern you); cosas así nunca sucedieron (these things never happened).

Verbs expressing acts of animals are not used normally in the first person: Yo ladro (I bark). But of course they can be used in a figurative sense: yo ladraba de hambre (I was barking due to being so hungry).

General List of Irregular Verbs

A list of some 600 verbs is given in the following pages. To include in it all the irregular Spanish verbs that could be heard or read in Mexico was a serious endeavor. That is why many verbs that appear in the lists of ENGEL, BELLO and other grammars and dictionaries, which are actually unknown or out of use (alebrarse, desflocar, dolar, enhestar, etc., etc., etc.) were excluded.

It was considered unnecessary and useless to include the NI verbs ending in llir, ñer and ñir that are otherwise regular (bullir, tañer, gruñir, etc.). The five verbs (abrir, cubrir, escribir, imprimir and romper) and their compound verbs, that are perfectly regular in their whole conjugation, save their irregular past participle, were not included either.

Maybe it was unnecessary to include 92 verbs ending in ecer (acontecer, amanecer, aparecer, etc.), because it is known that any verb with this ending, except mecer only, follows the GU irregularity. But they were included.

On the other hand, about 25 verbs which are absolutely regular (and are specially marked with R) were included. These verbs, for some reason or another, could be thought to be irregular. For instance, pretender is R, although all the other verbs ending in tender are DI (atiendo, contiendo), etc.). Ofender is R and its opposite defender is DI. Innovar is R and renovar is DI.

The great majority of the Spanish verbs are irregular in the present only, and all the irregular verbs (with the only exception of andar) have at least an irregular Yo Pres. For this reason, in my list:

One abbreviation after a verb (caer GU) means that such a verb is irregular in the present only (Yo Pres caigo).

Two abbreviations (pedir VO VO) mean that such a verb is irregular in the present and also in the past (Yo Pres pido, Els Pas pidieron).

Three abbreviations (hacer GU PI FI) mean, of course, that such a verb is irregular in the present, in the past and in the future (Yo Pres hago, Els Pas hicieron, Tu Fu harás).

A double abbreviation (oír GUYE) (traer GU PINI) means that such a verb has a double irregularity in the respective tense (Yo Pres GU oigo, Tu Pres YE oyes) (Yo Pres GU traigo, Els Pas PI and NI traj. ieron).

Almost always compound verbs have the same irregularity as their corresponding single verbs. In the General List a dot in the middle of a verb (abs.traer) means that such a verb is conjugated with the same irregularity or irregularities as the simple verb (traer).

A special mark (#) before a verb means that this infinitive is a simple verb which is never used this way without a prefix (#ducir, #cluir, #ferir, etc.)

General List of Irregular Verbs

abastecer GU	caer GU	#cordar DI	des.oír	enflaquecer GU
aborrecer GU	calentar DI	cornar DI	de.solar	enfurecer GU
abrogar R	carecer GU	cor.regir	de.soldar	engrandecer GU
ab.solver	cegar DI	corroer R	desollar DI	engreír VO VONI
abs.tener(se)	ceñir VO VONI	costar DI	des.pedir	enloquecer GU
abs.traer	cerner(se) DI	crecer GU	despertar DI	en.lucir
acaecer GU	cernir DI	dar MO MO R	des.plegar	en.mendar
a.certar GU	cerrar DI	de.caer	des.poblar	enmohecer GU
aco.medir(se)	#certar DI	decir GUVU PINI FI	des.templar	enmudecer GU
acontecer	cimentar DI	de.crecer	des.teñir	ennegrecer GU
a.cordar(se)	circuir YE	de.ducir	des.terrar	ennoblecer GU
a.costar(se)	#cluir YE	defender DI	des.tituir	enorgullecerse GU
acrecentar DI	cocer DI	de.ferir	des.tercer	enrarecer GU
ad.herir	colar DI	degollar DI	destronar R	enriquecer GU
adolecer GU	co.legir	de.moler	de.struir	enrojecer GU
adormecer GU	colgar DI	de.mostrar	desvanecer(se)	enronquecer GU
adquirir DI	co.medir(se)	de.negar	desvergonzarse DI	ensangrentar DI
a.ducir	comentar R	denostar DI	des.vestir	ensobercer GU
ad.vertir	comenzar DI	de.poner	de.tener	ensordecer GU
a.fluir	com. padecer	derogar R	de.traer	en.tender

agorar DI	com.parecer	derrengar DI	de.venir	enternecer GU
agradecer GU	compensar R	derretir VO VO	de.volver	en.terrar
agredir R	com.petir	derrocar	di.ferir	entontecer GU
alentar DI	com.placer	derruir YE	digerir DIVO VO	entorpecer GU
almorzar DI	com.poner	desaforar DI	di.luir	entre.cerrar
amanecer GU	com.probar	des.agradecer	discernir DI	entregar R
amolar DI	concebir VO VO	des.alentar	dis.cordar	entre.oír
andar R PI R	concernir Di R	des.andar	di.sentir	entre.tener
anegar DI o R	con.certar	des.aparecer	disminuir YE	entre.ver
anochecer GU	con.cluir	desa.probar	di.solver	entristecer GU
ante.poner	con.cordar	desa.sosegar	di.sonar	entumecerse GU
apacentar	conde. scender	desa.tender	dispensar R	envanecerse GU
a.parecer	con. doler(se)	desa.venir	dis.poner	envejecer GU
apetecer GU	con.ducir	de.scender	dis.tender	envilecer GU
apostar DI	con.ferir	des.ceñir	dis.traer	en.vovler
apretar DI	confesar DI	des.colgar	dis.tribuir	equi.valer
a.probar	con.fluir	descollar DI	divergir R	erguir DIVO VO
argüir YE	con.mover	desco.medir(se)	di.verter	errar DI (yerro)
arrendar DI	conocer GU	descom.poner	doler DI	escarmentar DI
arrepentirse DIVO VO	con.seguir	descon.centrar	dormir DIVO VO	escarnecer GU
arrogarse R	con.sentir	des.conocer	#ducir GU PINI	esclarecer GU
a.scender	con.solar	descon.solar	e.legir	es.cocer
a.sentar	con.sonar	des.contar	embellecer GU	es.forzar(se)

a.sentir	con.stituir	descon.venir	embestir VO VO	establecer GU
aserrar DI	constreñir VO VONI	des.cornar	embravecer GU	estar MO PI R
asir GU	con.struir	des.decir	embrutecer GU	estatuir YE
a.solar	contar DI	des.empedrar	emparentar DI	estregar DI
a.sonar	con.tender	desen.cerrar	empedrar DI	estremecer GU
atardecer GU	con.tener	desen. tender(se)	empequeñecer GU	estreñir VO VONI
a.tender	contentar R	desen.terrar	empezar DI	ex.cluir
a.tener(se)	con. torcer(se)	desen.volver	empobrecer GU	ex.pedir
atentar R	contra.decir	des.fallecer	enaltecer GU	ex.poner
aterrar R	con.traer	des.favorecer	enardecer GU	ex.tender
a.traer	contra. hacer	des.gobernar	encalvecer GU	ex.traer
atravesar DI	contra. poner	des.hacer	encallecer GU	fallecer GU
a.tribuir	contra.venir	desleír VO VONI	encanecer GU	favorecer GU
a.tronar	con.tribuir	des.lucir	encender DI	fenecer GU
a.venir(se)	contro. verter	des.medir(se)	en.cerrar	florecer GU
a.ventar	convalecer	desmembrar DI	enco.mendar	fluir YE
avergonzar(se) DI	von.venir	des.mentir	encontrar DI	#ferir DIVO VO
benderi GUVO PINI	convergir R	des.merecer	encrudecer GU	fortalecer GU
caber GU PI FI	con.vertir	des.obedecer	endurecer GU	forzar DI
fregar DI	#mendar DI	profesar R	re.producir	sosegar DI
freír VO VONI	mentar DI	pro.mover	re.quebrar	sos.tener
gemir VO VO	mentir DIVO VO	pro.poner	requerir DIVO VO	so.terrar
gobernar DI	merecer GU	prorrogar R	re.sentir	#stituir YE

guarecer GU	merendar DI	pro.seguir	re.solver	#struir YE
guarnecer GU	moler DI	pro.stituir	resollar DI	sub.arrendar
haber MO PI FI	morder DI	proveer R	re.sonar	suben.tender
hacer GU PI FI	morir DIVO VO	pro.venir	resplandecer GU	sub.seguir
heder DI	mostrar DI	pudrir R	restablecer GU	sub.venir
helar DI	mover DI	quebrar DI	re.stituir	sub.verter
henchir VO VO	nacer GU	querer DI PI FI	r.estregar	sugerir DIVO VO
hender DI	negar DI	raer GU	re.temblar	sumergir R
hendir DI	nevar DI	reblandecer GU	re.tener	super.poner
herir DIVO VO	obedecer GU	re.caer	re.tentar	su.poner
herrar DI	ob.struir	re.calentar	re.teñir	su.stituir
hervir DIVO VO	ob.tener	re.cluir	re.torecer	sus.traer
holgar DI	o.cluir	re.cocer	re.traer	temblar DI
hollar DI	ofender R	reco.mendar	re.tribuir	templar R
huir YE	ofrecer GU	recom.poner	retro.traer	tender DI
humedecer GU	oír GUYE	re.conocer	re.venir(se)	tener GUDI PI FI
imbuir YE	oler DU (huelo)	recon.stituir	re.ventar	tenar DI
im.pedir	o.poner	recon.struir	re.ver	teñir VO VONI
im.poner	oscurecer	re.contar	reverdecer GU	#terrar DI
incensar DI	pacer	recon.venir	re.verter	torcer DI
inc.luir	padecer GU	re.cordar	re.vertir	tostar DI
indis.poner	palidecer GU	re.costar(se)	re.vestir	tra.ducir
in.ducir	parecer GU	recrudecer GU	re.volar	traer GU PINI
in.ferir	pedir VO VO	red.argüir	re.volcar	trans.ferir
in.fluir	pensar DI	re.ducir	re.volver	transgredir R

ingerir DIVO VO	perder DI	ree.legir	robustecer GU	tra.scender
injerir DIVO VO	perecer GU	reex.pedir	rodar DI	tras.colar
inmiscuir YE	permanecer GU	re.ferir	roer R o GU	tras.cordar(se)
innovar R	perni. quebrar	re.fluir	rogar DI	trasegar DI
inquirir DI	per.seguir	re.forzar	saber GU PI FI	tras.lucir
in.stituir	pertenecer GU	re.fregar	salir GU R FI	tras.poner
in.struir	per.vertir	re.freír	satisfacer GU PI FI	tras.tocar
inter.ferir	#petir VO VO	rogar DI	#scender DI	tras.volar
inter.poner	placer GU	regir VO VO	se.ducir	tra.vestir
inter.venir	plastecer GU	regoldar DI	segar DI	#tribuir YE
intro.ducir	plegar DI	re.hacer	seguir VO VO	trocar DI
intuir YE	poblar DI	re.henchir	sembrar DI	tronar DI
in.vertir	poder DI PI FI	re.huir	sentar DI	tropezar DI
in.vestir	podrir (pudrir)	reír VO VONI	sentir DIVO VO	valer GU R FI
ir MO MO R	poner GU PI FI	rejuvenecer GU	ser MO MO R	venir GUDI PI FI
jugar DI	pos.poner	re.lucir	servir VO VO	#ventar DI
languidecer GU	pre.concebir	re.mendar	sobren.tender	ver MO MO R
#legir VO VO	pre.decir	re.moler	sobre.poner	verter DI
lucir GU	predis. poner	re.morder	sobre.salir	#verter DIVO VO
luir YE	pre.ferir	re.mover	sobre.venir	vestir VO VO
llover DI	presentar R	re.nacer	so.freír	volar DI
maldecir GUVO PINI	pre.sentir	rendir VO VO	#solar DI	volcar DI
mal.herir	presu.poner	re.negar	soldar DI	volver DI

mal.querer	pretender R	re.novar	soler DI	yacer GU
mal.traer	pre.valecer GU	reñir VO VONI	soltar DI	yuxta.poner
man.cornar	pre.venir	re.petir	#solver DI	za.herir
manifestar DI	pre.ver	re.plegar	sonar DI	
man.tener	probar DI	re.poblar	son.reir	
mecer R	pro.ducir	re.poner	soñar DI	
medir VO VO	pro.ferir	re.probar	sorber R	